Love Matters

A Christian Guide to Staying in Love or Falling in Love Again With Your Partner

Mark David Albertson

Irish Viking
publishing

IRISH VIKING PUBLISHING

Book Cover by Chad Gupta

Contents

To every couple who has ever whispered, "I love you," and then immediately wondered how on earth love can feel so beautiful, complicated, hilarious, exhausting, and holy all at once.

May these pages feel like a hand on your shoulder,

a gentle nudge toward grace,

and a reminder that love is not something you master —

it's something you practice.

And to my beloved Kaia...

Life makes more sense when you're standing beside me.

Thank you for being the truest thing in my world.

Forward

If you had told me twenty-five years ago that I would one day write a book on marriage — a book meant to encourage couples, guide them, comfort them, challenge them, and maybe even make them laugh — I would've smiled politely and then asked if you were feeling well.

But here I am.

Writing a marriage book.

And doing it with more humility, honesty, and hard-earned wisdom than I ever expected to have.

Before I go any further, let me confess something right up front:

I've been married three times.

Not once.

Not twice.

Three.

Some people write marriage books because they believe they've mastered marriage.

I'm writing this book because I've lived enough life to know no one ever truly masters it — we simply keep learning, keep growing, and keep choosing love in all its complicated, beautiful forms.

If you're wondering, "Well then what qualifies you to guide anyone else?"

Here's my answer:

Grace. Experience. And a lifelong calling to help people reconcile — with each other, with God, and with themselves.

For years I served as a pastor. I sat with couples in their joy and in their heartbreak, in their wedding planning and in their "we don't know what else to do" moments. Before that, I was the Director of the Christian Conciliation Service of Puget Sound — a ministry dedicated to helping people repair relationships, resolve conflict, and rediscover hope where hope had been almost extinguished.

I've spent a lifetime listening to real people tell real stories about real love —

the kind of love that doesn't always look neat and tidy,

the kind of love that goes to counseling,

the kind of love that survives apologies and rebuilds trust,

the kind of love that ages and learns and softens with time.

And I've written for much of my life — stories, devotionals, studies, reflections — all with one goal: to make faith feel less like a performance and more like a journey we're all learning to walk.

So yes, I've been married three times.

Yes, I've made mistakes.

And yes, I've loved deeply — imperfectly, but truly.

Those experiences have shaped me, humbled me, and pushed me to write a book that refuses to pretend marriage is easy... but absolutely insists it can be good.

Who This Book Is For

This book is for couples who are brand new and trying to figure out how to build something meaningful from day one.

It's for couples who are struggling — the ones who still love each other but feel stuck, tired, discouraged, or confused about how to move forward.

It's for couples who are doing well but want to go deeper — wanting more connection, more grace, more intentionality, more joy.

It's for couples of every configuration — heterosexual, same-sex, newly partnered, long-time married, engaged, remarried, reconciling, or rediscovering each other after life threw a few curveballs.

It's for pastors and church leaders who walk alongside couples during the joyful and messy chapters of their lives.

It's for Christian marriage counselors and spiritual companions who need practical, grace-filled tools they can use with clients or congregants.

And yes — it's for that person who quietly picks up this book thinking, "I hope this helps my friend."

What This Book Is (and Isn't)

This book is not a theological treatise or a list of magical formulas to guarantee marital bliss. It's not an instruction manual from someone pretending to have all the answers.

Instead, it's a workbook — something you and your partner can actually use.

Talk through.

Reflect on.

Return to.

It's intentionally practical, intentionally spiritual, and intentionally honest.

There are 30 chapters, each focusing on one essential theme:

communication

conflict

forgiveness

listening

emotional safety

spiritual connection

tenderness

gratitude

and so much more

Each chapter is designed to be read and discussed in less than an hour — short enough for busy couples, meaningful enough to spark transformation.

Every chapter includes:

a real conversation about a real topic

personal stories

spiritual grounding

reflection questions

and a small, doable homework practice

Some chapters will make you laugh.

Some may make you cry.

Some will feel like warm encouragement.

Others may feel like a gentle nudge.

All of them, I hope, will help you see each other more clearly and love each other more deeply.

My Hope for You

I wrote this book because I believe marriage — at its best — is one of the most sacred, vulnerable, courageous, and transformative relationships we can experience. It stretches us. It refines us. It reveals us. And yes, sometimes it exposes the places in us that still need healing.

But it also blesses us.

It comforts us.

It anchors us.

It teaches us to show grace the way God shows grace.

It gives us a partner in life, in growth, in faith, in humor, and in the everyday moments that make a life.

My hope is that these thirty chapters help you know your partner better.

Help you articulate what you need.

Help you practice love in tangible ways.

Help you fight fair, apologize well, reconnect often, and choose grace freely.

Whether your marriage is brand new, beautifully established, struggling, or somewhere in between — this book is for you.

Because love matters.

And your relationship matters.

And you deserve a resource that meets you in the real world — with honesty, tenderness, and hope.

So take a deep breath.

Grab a pen.

Sit down with your partner.

Let's begin this journey — one meaningful, imperfect, grace-filled step at a time.

Chapter One

LOVE MATTERS: WHY WE START HERE

Every marriage begins with a moment — sometimes dramatic, sometimes quiet, sometimes surprisingly awkward — when two people look at each other and think, "Okay, wow. It's you. You're my person." It might happen on a first date, or a third date, or eight months into a friendship when you suddenly realize you're staring at their face like it's a sunrise and thinking, Huh. I would rearrange my entire life for this goofball.

That moment, whatever it looked like for you, is beautiful.

Sacred, even.

And it really, truly matters.

But as anyone who has been married longer than fifteen minutes can tell you, that moment — that spark — is not enough to build a life on. It's a great beginning. A wonderful beginning. A beginning worthy of commemorating with a scrapbook, a photo, or at least a story you exaggerate every year until neither of you can remember what actually happened.

But beginnings don't make marriages. Daily choices do. And the first daily choice is this: love matters.

It matters when you're tired.

It matters when you're stressed.

It matters when your partner says something baffling, or leaves their shoes in the exact spot you trip over every single day, or forgets that you told them about that thing... twice. Okay, three times.

Love matters especially on the days when it doesn't feel glamorous, Instagrammable, or worthy of a Hallmark movie.

Because if you stay married long enough, you discover something both comforting and mildly terrifying:

Love is less about the *feeling*

and more about the *choosing*.

That's why we're starting this book here — not with communication techniques, or conflict tools, or even forgiveness. Those things are important, of course. They'll show up in later chapters like helpful guests bringing casseroles to the party. But the very first ingredient, the essential one, the one that makes all the others possible is this:

You choose to love your partner, and you keep choosing them even when it's hard.

Not "hard" like climbing Mount Everest.

Hard like getting misunderstood.

Hard like differing on finances.

Hard like seeing their flaws — and your own — up close.

Hard like having to say, "I didn't handle that well," or "Wow, I think I'm crankier than I realized."

Love matters because love sees the whole person — the brilliant parts, the complicated parts, the growing parts — and decides, "Yep. Them. I'm in."

The Myth of Effortless Love

There's this myth floating around out there — looking suspiciously like it came from rom-coms and people who have never shared a bathroom with another adult — that true love should always feel effortless.

If it's meant to be, it should be easy.

If it's the right person, it should never feel like work.

If you were soulmates, you would always agree, always laugh, always kiss at sunset.

Let me be very pastoral with you for a moment:

Nope. No. Absolutely not.

Real love is not effortless.

Real love requires showing up.

Sometimes repeatedly.

Sometimes after you've taken a walk around the block muttering to yourself.

Real love is not the absence of struggle —

it's the decision to stay tender in the middle of it.

Effort doesn't mean something's wrong.

Effort means something matters.

Meet Jonah and Priya

Jonah and Priya met at a salsa class. Jonah had the rhythm of an overcaffeinated penguin, but Priya liked that he tried enthusiastically anyway. Their first few dates were electric — the kind of thing you tell your friends about with animated hand gestures. They were smitten. Butterflies. Fireworks. But with less danger.

Six months into marriage, however, the choreography looked different. They argued about dishes. They argued about how to fold towels (Priya's way was objectively better). They argued about whether Jonah "listened" or whether he "heard noise while thinking about something else entirely."

One night, after a long day and a short fuse, they sat on the couch, staring at each other in exhausted silence. Priya finally said, "Is it supposed to be this... difficult sometimes?"

Jonah hesitated, then said the truest thing either of them had said in weeks:

"I still choose us. Even when it's hard."

And the tension softened.

Not because everything was suddenly fixed,

but because they remembered something essential:

Love is not magic.

Love is commitment in motion.

They weren't failing.

They were simply learning how to love each other in real time.

The Courage to Love Imperfectly

Loving someone means letting them see the real you — not the curated version, not the "company's coming over" version, but the version who gets overwhelmed, gets insecure, gets impatient, gets distracted, gets discouraged, and occasionally gets Snickers-hungry.

Your partner didn't marry perfection.

They married *you*.

And you are a gift — even when you're growing, even when you're learning, even when you're stumbling toward grace.

True love doesn't require perfection.

But it absolutely requires courage.

The courage to say,

"I'm still in this, even when I don't have my act together."

The courage to believe,

"You're still in this with me, even when your rough edges poke me a little."

The courage to trust that two imperfect humans can build something strong, beautiful, and lasting — not because they always get it right, but because they refuse to stop trying.

Love Is a Daily Practice

If you think of marriage as a giant performance, you'll constantly feel like you're falling short. But if you think of marriage as a daily practice, something shifts.

Love becomes something you do, not something you feel.

You practice kindness.

You practice patience.

You practice listening.

You practice forgiveness.

You practice tenderness when you're tired.

You practice asking for what you need without apology.

You practice celebrating your partner's small victories.

You practice returning to each other after conflict.

You practice the tiny gestures that say:

"Hey, I'm here. I'm choosing you again today."

Love becomes a habit — not automatic, but intentional.

And the more you practice, the deeper it becomes.

Why Love Still Matters (Even on the Hard Days)

There will be mornings when you feel fully connected — like your hearts are synced up on the same spiritual Wi-Fi. You'll laugh easily. You'll finish each other's sentences. You'll feel profoundly blessed.

There will also be mornings when you look at your partner and think,

"We are not on the same wavelength. Are you even on the same planet right now?"

Both days are normal.

Both days belong in a marriage.

Both days are opportunities to choose love again.

And that's the secret:

Love matters because it transforms ordinary humans into partners, teammates, companions, and co-creators of a shared life.

It matters because it keeps pulling you toward each other.

It matters because it keeps your hearts soft.

It matters because it gives you the resilience to try again.

It matters because life will absolutely throw things at you — and love is what allows you to face them together instead of alone.

Reflection Questions

Think back to when you first knew your partner mattered to you. What made that moment feel significant?

What are three small ways you practice love on an ordinary Tuesday?

Which parts of love come easily to you? Which require more intentionality?

How does it feel to think of love as something you choose rather than something you "fall into"?

What does "love matters" mean to you today, in this season of your relationship?

Homework for Chapter One

1. The Love Story Exchange

Sit together and take turns sharing the moment you knew this relationship was real. Don't rush it. Let yourself remember.

2. One Small Act Today

Each of you chooses one tiny act of kindness to do today — something that whispers, "You matter to me."

3. A Simple Prayer (Optional, but beautiful)

"God, help us choose love again and again."

Chapter Two

THE POWER OF BEING KNOWN

There's a moment in every serious relationship when you realize something quietly astonishing:

This person... sees me.

Maybe it happens when they remember the oddly specific way you like your coffee. Or when they instinctively know your "thinking face" versus your "please don't talk to me yet" face. Or when you say, "I'm fine," and they respond with the soft, gentle, "No... you're not." And somehow you don't feel offended — you feel understood.

Being known is one of the deepest human desires we carry. From childhood all the way into adulthood, we're all hungry to be seen — not just observed, but recognized. To be understood not only by our behavior, but by our heart.

In marriage/partnership, this longing takes on even greater weight. Because if you're going to share a home, a life, a bed, a budget, a family, and sometimes a Netflix account with someone, you want to believe you're not invisible in your own story.

And yet, as beautiful as being known is... it's also terrifying.

Because to be known, you have to be seen.

To be seen, you have to be honest.

To be honest, you have to let someone close.

And letting someone close means letting them see things you might not even like about yourself.

Marriage is where your real self eventually shows up — the tired self, the anxious self, the tender self, the self that sometimes gets overwhelmed by too many decisions at Costco. And here's the gift:

Being known isn't about perfection.

It's about authenticity.

And authenticity, while terrifying, is also the birthplace of intimacy.

Meet Daniel and Simone

Daniel and Simone had been together for almost two years when Simone realized something wasn't quite connecting. It wasn't that Daniel wasn't kind — he was. And not that he wasn't attentive — he was that too, at least in the big-picture ways. But whenever she asked how he was feeling, he would respond with something vague like:

"I'm okay."

or

"It's fine."

or

"You know… just stuff."

Stuff?

What stuff?

What specific emotional flavor of "stuff" are we working with here, Daniel?

Simone wanted to know him — *really* know him. She could sense the layers beneath the surface, but he guarded them like a museum curator protecting the last dinosaur egg.

Finally, one night she sat down next to him and asked gently, "Do you trust me with the real you?" She said it without accusation, without pressure, just quiet curiosity.

Daniel stared at the floor for a long moment before whispering something he had never said out loud to anyone:

"I don't know how."

He wasn't being dramatic. He wasn't hiding on purpose. He had grown up in a family where emotions were treated like hazardous materials — handle with gloves, store in a locked container, and never under any circumstances open them in front of other people. Vulnerability wasn't safe. Transparency wasn't practiced. Honesty wasn't encouraged; it was punished.

He had learned to survive by being quiet.

And Simone — to her credit — didn't push. She didn't say, "Well, you better figure it out." She simply said, "Okay. Then we'll learn together."

That's when everything shifted.

Not overnight.

Not instantly.

But slowly, gently, beautifully.

Daniel started practicing tiny revelations: "Today was stressful." "I felt discouraged at work." "I'm afraid of letting you down." Simone received each truth like a sacred offering — with tenderness, not judgment.

Over time, he learned this truth many of us learn late:

Being known isn't dangerous

when you're loved well.

The Levels of Knowing Someone

We tend to think being known means revealing everything at once — a sort of emotional dump truck of childhood wounds, secret longings, fears, hopes, insecurities, and confessions. But being known is actually built in layers.

The surface layer

This is what your coworkers know: "Oh yeah, he likes baseball," or "She's allergic to pecans and mornings."

The preference layer

Your partner knows how you take your coffee, which songs make you emotional, and how to interpret your "I'm overwhelmed" shoulder shrug.

The emotional layer

This is where your partner knows what hurts you, what delights you, what scares you, and what lights you up from the inside.

The sacred layer

This is the deepest one — your fears, your stories, your spiritual journey, the private ache you rarely name, and the prayer you whisper when you're not sure God is listening.

Being known is the slow unveiling of all four layers — not rushed, not forced, but shared in the safety of love.

Why We Hide Ourselves

There are a few common reasons people struggle to be known:

1. Fear of rejection

"What if you don't love the real me?"

2. Shame

"What if I show you something tender and you judge me?"

3. Past wounds

"What if you hurt me the way someone else did?"

4. Performance pressure

"What if I'm not as impressive as you think I am?"

Here's the truth your marriage needs:

Your partner didn't fall in love with your performance.

They fell in love with you.

And they want the real version — the one with layers, texture, contradictions, dreams, and flaws.

The Grace of Being Known Imperfectly

You don't have to reveal everything perfectly. You don't have to always explain yourself clearly. You just have to be willing to let your partner glimpse what's true about you.

Sometimes you'll get it right.

Sometimes you'll say it clumsily and wish you could hit "undo."

Sometimes you'll learn things about yourself in the middle of the conversation.

And sometimes you'll surprise each other in beautiful ways.

Being known doesn't mean telling your partner everything at once.

It means letting them walk beside you while you figure yourself out.

How to Know Your Partner More Deeply

Here are a few tools — conversational, not mechanical — for creating deeper knowing in your marriage:

1. Ask curious questions

Not interrogation. Not therapy. Just gentle curiosity:

"What was the best part of your day?"

"What's been on your mind lately?"

"What do you wish people understood about you?"

"What's something you're longing for right now?"

Curiosity is the spark that keeps intimacy glowing.

2. Listen for what's beneath the words

Tone carries truth.

Silence carries truth.

A sigh carries truth.

A pause sometimes says more than a paragraph.

3. Validate, don't fix

Sometimes the best response to your partner's vulnerability is simply:

"That makes sense."

or

"Thank you for telling me."

People open up when they feel safe.

4. Open up in small steps

You don't have to jump off the emotional cliff.

Just wade in.

Share one small thought today, one fear tomorrow, one dream next week. Let your partner earn trust through tenderness.

The Sacredness of Being Known

Spiritually speaking, being known is one of the most profound experiences we can have. Scripture reminds us again and again that God knows us intimately — the hairs on our head, the quietest thoughts, the deepest fears, the longings we barely articulate.

When you allow your partner to know you, you are practicing that same kind of sacred trust.

You are saying, "Here I am. Not perfect. Not polished. But real."

And when your partner holds that truth with gentleness, it becomes a holy moment — the kind of moment marriages are built on.

Reflection Questions

What parts of yourself do you find easiest to share with your partner?

Which parts feel more guarded, and why?

In what moments do you feel most "seen" by your partner?

What helps you feel safe enough to be known?

What would it look like for you to know your partner even more deeply?

Homework for Chapter Two

1. The Knowing Game

Take turns answering three questions:

"What's one thing you wish people knew about you?"

"What's one thing that brings you comfort?"

"What's something you're dreaming about lately?"

2. One Small Vulnerable Sentence

Each of you shares a single sentence beginning with:

"I haven't said this before, but..."

Keep it gentle. Keep it small.

3. Pray (or breathe) together for openness

"God, help us know each other more deeply and love each other more fully."

Chapter Three

THE MINISTRY OF SMALL THINGS

If love had a filing cabinet in heaven, it probably wouldn't be labeled with grand gestures, epic speeches, or surprise trips to Paris. It would be filled with tiny acts of kindness — the ones done on Tuesday mornings before coffee, or late at night when no one feels poetic, or in the middle of making dinner while the dog is barking and someone can't find the scissors they literally just had in their hand.

Small things are the backbone of marriage.

Always have been.

Always will be.

Because in the real world — the non-movie world — a strong marriage is built less on fireworks and more on flickering candles that stay lit year after year.

These small things may not look like much from the outside, but inside a marriage, they're monumental. They say:

"I see you."

"I'm with you."

"You matter."

"You're worth this moment."

And they say all of that without you needing to book a resort weekend or orchestrate a flash mob.

Love thrives in the subtle, the steady, the ordinary.

And ordinary, it turns out, can be sacred.

Meet Marco and Devon

Marco and Devon were deeply in love, wonderfully committed, and absolutely terrible at loading the dishwasher the same way.

Marco believed the dishwasher was a precision instrument requiring NASA-level strategy: plates angled for optimal spray reach, utensils sorted like soldiers, bowls arranged as if participating in synchronized swimming.

Devon... did not share this spiritual calling.

Devon loaded the dishwasher like a jazz musician — improvisational, bold, free-form, confident that the water would find its way somehow.

This difference led to many evenings of teeth-clenching. Marco would "fix" the dishwasher after Devon loaded it, and Devon would feel secretly judged by the invisible dishwasher police.

One Tuesday night — a night not special for any reason except that grace decided to show up — Marco walked into the kitchen, saw the dishwasher loaded in its usual Devon style, and reached for the handle to redo it.

Then he paused.

And did something radical.

He closed the door.

Pressed "Start."

And walked away.

Devon noticed.

Not the dishwasher — but the absence of commentary.

And oddly enough, that tiny moment, that unlikely, unglamorous decision, became a turning point in their marriage. Because Marco learned something that night:

Sometimes love looks like letting the dishwasher be chaotic.

Sometimes love looks like letting your partner be human.

It was a small thing.

But it changed everything.

Why the Small Things Matter So Much

Small acts don't always seem impressive, but they are incredibly powerful because they accumulate. Each one builds emotional trust, fosters connection, and creates a shared rhythm of kindness.

It's like spiritual compound interest.

Little deposits, over time, build something huge.

Small acts matter because they:

Create stability. You don't have to wonder if your partner cares — they show you daily.

Break tension before it escalates. A tiny kindness can stop resentment from taking root.

Make the ordinary feel intentional. And when the ordinary becomes meaningful, life gets sweeter.

Say what words sometimes can't:

I love you in this moment, as it is, without needing it to be more glamorous.

Big gestures are wonderful, but they are seasonal.

Small gestures are daily bread.

The Holiness of the Ordinary

If you look at the Gospels, Jesus spent far more time doing small things than big ones.

He walked with people.

Listened to people.

Shared meals.

Touched wounds.

Called people by name.

Showed up in their everyday lives.

Miracles were few and far between.

Small actions? Constant.

This is good news for marriage, because it means your daily actions — whether sacred or mundane — can become spiritual practices when done with love.

A marriage built on dramatic gestures alone is like a house made of fireworks. Exciting, yes. Sustainable? Not so much.

But a marriage built on tiny acts of gentleness?

That's where the good stuff grows.

Examples of Small Things That Mean Everything

Here are a few tiny, unglamorous acts that can build a mountain of love over time:

- Making their coffee the way they like it.

- Setting aside the last cookie even when you wanted it.

- Letting them sleep in.

- Saying "thank you" for the ordinary tasks.

- Putting your phone down when they're talking.

- Bringing them water before bed.

- Sending a random "thinking of you" text.

- Warming up the car.

- Asking, "How can I make your day easier?"

- Taking over a chore without being asked.

- Giving a hug that's two seconds longer than usual.

These aren't dramatic.

Nobody's making a movie about them.

But these tiny things?

They are relationship oxygen.

The Five-Second Rule

Here's a simple practice that can transform even the busiest marriage:

If you can do something in five seconds that makes your partner's life easier... do it.

- Pick up the socks.

- Rinse the mug.

- Toss the trash.

- Close the cabinet they left open (again).

- Send that "hope you're doing okay" text.

- Refill the ice tray (the least glamorous act of love on

earth).

These five-second gestures whisper,

"I'm thinking of you. I'm in this with you."

And whispers, over time, become a chorus.

Small Acts During Hard Seasons

Sometimes the small things matter most during the hardest seasons. When stress is high, when grief is present, when you're overwhelmed or discouraged, tiny acts become lifelines.

- A gentle back rub.

- A warm meal.

- A blanket placed around shoulders.

- A soft, "Let me take care of this tonight."

These small acts say,

"You don't have to hold everything alone."

And that is the kind of love that saves people.

Reflection Questions

What small acts from your partner make you feel most loved?

What simple gesture could you add into your daily rhythm that your partner might appreciate?

Which small acts are easy for you to give? Which are harder?

What small action could you try this week to soften a tense moment?

How have small things shaped your relationship so far?

Homework for Chapter Three

1. The Seven-Day Small Act Challenge

Every day this week, choose one tiny, concrete thing you can do to bless your partner — something that takes under a minute but carries meaning.

2. Notice the Small Things

Each of you writes down five small things your partner does that you appreciate. Exchange lists.

3. A Simple Sanctuary Moment

Tonight, take 60 seconds to sit quietly together — holding hands, breathing, resting. No agenda. Just presence.

Chapter Four

SEEING YOUR PARTNER AS BELOVED

There's a moment in the Gospels that still gives me goose-bumps every time I picture it. Jesus comes up out of the Jordan River — wet hair, shivering a little, probably smelling like fish and river moss — and God's voice breaks through the sky with a declaration so tender it feels like a heartbeat:

"You are my beloved. With you I am well pleased."

Beloved.

It's one of those words you don't use casually. It holds weight, warmth, and a kind of sacred softness. And here's the wild part: that's how God feels about every human being.

Including the one you married.

Your partner — with all their quirks, flaws, moods, history, and unwashed coffee mugs — is someone God calls beloved long before you ever met them. Long before you had your first date.

Long before you exchanged vows. Long before they borrowed your sweatshirt and never returned it.

And learning to see your partner the way God sees them may be the most transformational shift in a marriage.

Because once you begin practicing it, everything else changes: the patience you offer, the grace you extend, the tenderness you choose, the way you interpret their flaws, and even how you forgive.

Seeing your partner as beloved means remembering: "This human in front of me is precious. Sacred. Worthy. Cherished. Even on the days we annoy each other."

The Theology of Human Annoyance

Let's be honest for a moment: in marriage, annoyance is unavoidable. It's not a sign of incompatibility — it's a sign you're two humans living close enough to see (and hear) each other's full humanity.

There will come a day when your partner chews too loudly.

Or breathes too loudly.

Or exists too loudly.

There will be days when you wonder if they've intentionally developed new noises just to test your sanctification.

That doesn't mean anything is wrong.

It means you are married.

Being annoyed is normal.

Being unkind is optional.

Seeing your partner as beloved creates enough internal space to let annoyance exist without letting it damage the relationship.

Because beneath the frustration, beneath the quirks, beneath the moments of "Why do you put the toilet paper on that way?" lies a sacred truth:

Your partner is beloved of God — even when they're flawed.

Even when they're grumpy.

Even when they are, for reasons known only to the heavens, loudly stirring their coffee at 6:00 a.m.

Meet Sarah and Lee

Sarah and Lee had been married for eleven years when they entered what they eventually titled "The Season of Sighing."

It wasn't dramatic sighing.

No, no — these were micro-sighs.

The sigh when Lee forgot to take the trash out.

The sigh when Sarah reorganized the spice cabinet again.

The sigh when Lee left the cupboard doors open like a poltergeist with organizational issues.

The sigh when Sarah wanted to talk at the exact moment Lee's brain needed to reboot.

Sigh.

Sigh.

Siiiiigh.

One night, after a particularly sigh-heavy day, Sarah sat on the couch scrolling through old photos — the ones from when their love was new, and everything felt like magic. She saw their younger faces, their bright eyes, their goofy expressions, and she felt her heart soften.

She turned to Lee and said quietly, "I think I've forgotten how beloved you are."

And Lee, who was feeling frustrated too, let out a long breath — not a micro-sigh this time, but the kind that comes right before a miracle — and replied, "Yeah. Me too."

They sat together for a long moment. No lecture, no analysis, no dramatic vows. Just two people remembering that they were more than roommates, more than co-parents, more than chore-sharing adults in a very loud world.

They were beloved.

And they had forgotten.

Remembering changed everything.

It didn't make the cupboard doors magically shut themselves.

But it made the sighs stop feeling like judgments.

It made the love feel deeper again.

It made the marriage feel holier.

Seeing the Child Within

One of the most compassionate mindshifts in marriage is remembering that your spouse carries every version of themselves
inside them: the child who wanted to be accepted

- the teenager who felt insecure

- the young adult who feared failure

- the hopeful dreamer

- the kid who used to laugh too loudly

- the version of them who wished someone would listen

- the one who prayed quietly at night, even when they
  weren't sure how prayer worked

Seeing your partner as beloved means seeing all of them — the
grown-up and the child beneath the grown-up — and meeting
both with tenderness.

Because often, the reactions that frustrate us most aren't reactions to the present moment. They're reactions shaped by past
wounds, unspoken fears, or the quiet ache of not wanting to
disappoint the person they love most.

When you see your partner this way, judgment softens.

Grace expands.

Compassion deepens.

You begin asking questions like,

"What's tender here?"

"What's underneath this reaction?"

"What might they be afraid of right now?"

That's what belovedness does — it invites curiosity instead of condemnation.

The Beloved Lens Changes Everything

Seeing your partner as beloved doesn't mean ignoring their flaws. It means seeing their flaws in context — not as evidence of failure, but as proof that they're human. Just like you.

It means:

- you speak with dignity, even in conflict

- you assume good intentions before assuming the worst

- you pray for them, not about them

- you celebrate every bit of growth, no matter how small

- you hold space for their fragility

- you stop expecting perfection, because belovedness is already enough

Belovedness reframes everything.

It turns partners into teammates.

It turns moments of frustration into opportunities for closeness.

It turns disagreements into invitations to deeper understanding.

The Practice of Seeing Each Other Clearly

Here are a few ways to put this into daily practice:

1. Imagine God speaking over your spouse.

"You are my beloved. With you I am well pleased."

Say it quietly in your heart. Let it change how you respond.

2. Look for glimpses of the child inside them.

When they're defensive, tired, or overwhelmed, imagine the younger version who once needed gentleness.

3. Speak blessings aloud.

"You matter to me."

"I'm proud of you."

"I'm glad you're my partner."

These are spiritual vitamins.

4. Practice soft eyes.

Soft eyes see beauty where irritation wants to take over.

Reflection Questions

When do you struggle most to see your partner as beloved?

When do you see it most easily?

What childhood wound or past experience might still influence their reactions today?

What would change if you practiced seeing them through God's eyes?

What affirmation could you speak over them this week?

Homework for Chapter Four

1. The Beloved Blessing

Place a hand on your partner's shoulder (or hold their hand) and say,

"I'm grateful for you. You are beloved."

Short, simple, powerful.

2. A Photo for the Heart

Look at a picture from early in your relationship.

Remember what drew you together.

3. A Quiet Prayer

"God, help me see my partner the way You see them."

Chapter Five

GRACE FOR TWO IMPERFECT PEOPLE

Here's a secret that should be printed on every marriage license in bold, glittery letters:

You married a human.

Not a superhero.

Not a mind reader.

Not a flawless creature woven together by angels and excellent boundaries.

Just a human — a beautifully complex, occasionally confusing, deeply emotional, sometimes inconsistent, often delightful human.

And guess what?

They married a human too.

Marriage is two imperfect people learning to show each other grace while simultaneously bumping into each other's rough edges, hidden fears, old wounds, morning breath, and moods that come out of nowhere like a rogue cloud on a sunny day.

Grace is not optional here.

Grace is the glue.

Imperfect Human #1 Meets Imperfect Human #2

It's easy to forget that you and your partner began your relationship with optimism, charm, and a nearly Olympic-level desire to impress each other.

But then... real life.

Suddenly the things you never noticed now have starring roles:

the way they leave shoes in mysterious places

the way they get quiet instead of talking

the forgotten grocery items

the late-night snacking

the tendency to assume the toilet paper refills itself via magic

the exact tone they use when they're "not upset" but also definitely a little bit upset

Your imperfections meet their imperfections,

and sparks fly —

sometimes the romantic kind,

sometimes the friction kind.

This is where grace becomes essential.

Not grace as in "I'm right and you're wrong, but I'll generously overlook it."

That's not grace.

That's ego in a fancy hat.

Grace is this:

I know you're flawed.

I know I am too.

Let's keep choosing each other anyway.

Meet Aisha and Sam

Aisha and Sam had been dating for a year before they married, and during that year everything felt smooth and harmonious. They were the couple everyone envied — rarely argued, always holding hands, finishing each other's sentences (sometimes incorrectly, but adorable nonetheless).

Six months into marriage, something shifted.

Not because they stopped loving each other,

but because they finally relaxed enough to be themselves.

Aisha discovered that Sam processed emotions slowly — like a thoughtful sloth with a theology degree. Sam discovered that Aisha processed emotions quickly — like a caffeinated prophet proclaiming truths at high speed.

One Thursday evening, this difference collided.

Aisha wanted to talk through an issue immediately.

Sam wanted time to think.

By "time," he meant about 36 hours.

By "talk," she meant approximately right now.

Voices didn't escalate.

But tension did.

Aisha felt abandoned.

Sam felt overwhelmed.

Both felt misunderstood.

That night, while brushing her teeth, Aisha realized something shocking: Sam wasn't doing anything wrong. He was simply doing something different.

And Sam — pacing in the living room with a cup of tea — realized that Aisha's intensity wasn't an attack; it was passion mixed with vulnerability.

They apologized, hugged, and then said the magic words that every marriage needs to keep stored in the silverware drawer for emergencies:

"We need more grace."

Not more perfection.

More grace.

From that moment on, they began practicing grace like it was a daily vitamin — small doses, taken often.

And slowly, their differences became less like landmines

and more like invitations to compassion.

Where Grace Matters Most

Grace is not weakness.

It's strength wrapped in gentleness.

And it's most powerful in the moments when your partner:

- says the wrong thing

- forgets something important

- gets overwhelmed

- shuts down

- reacts too quickly

- reacts too slowly

- leaves tasks half-finished

- gets cranky

- withdraws

- miscommunicates

- doesn't know what they need

- doesn't know what you need

Grace is what makes a marriage resilient instead of brittle.

Without grace, relationships fracture.

With grace, they bend and bounce back.

Grace doesn't mean enabling harmful behavior.

It doesn't mean ignoring real issues.

It means approaching real issues with softness, not sharpness.

Put simply:

Grace is truth spoken gently

and love offered consistently.

The Grace Gap

Every couple has what therapists call "the gap" — the space between who your partner is and who you imagined they would be.

Grace fills the gap.

Sometimes the gap is big ("I didn't know you disliked every vegetable except corn").

Sometimes the gap is small ("I didn't know you squeeze the toothpaste from the top, like a monster").

If you try to fix your partner into the version you imagined, the gap becomes a breeding ground for resentment.

If you fill the gap with grace,

the gap becomes a place where love grows deeper than expectations.

Grace says,

"You don't have to be the fantasy version for me to love you.

I choose the real you."

Giving Grace Without Losing Yourself

Grace is not self-abandonment.

It's not swallowing your needs.

It's not pretending everything is fine when it's not.

Grace is offering kindness while telling the truth.

It's balancing love and honesty.

It's saying, "I see you're struggling" and also "This hurt me."

It's holding boundaries with warmth, not ice.

Grace and truth are not opposites.

They're partners.

And healthy couples learn to use both.

Grace in the Daily Mess

Here are tiny, ordinary ways grace shows up:

Laughing off the small mistakes

Letting your partner try again when they mess up

Assuming good intentions

Being curious before being critical

Offering softness when their edges show

Giving each other room to have bad days

Saying "I know you didn't mean it that way"

Choosing patience when you could choose irritation

Grace doesn't erase imperfection.

It honors it.

It softens it.

It welcomes it with kindness.

The Spiritual Side of Grace

Grace is woven through the entire Christian story:

God chooses imperfect people

God heals broken places

God forgives

God restores

God loves before we earn anything

When you extend grace in your marriage, you echo the heart of God.

You say with your actions what Scripture says with beauty:

"Love covers a multitude of sins."

—not by ignoring them, but by *healing* them.

Grace is how we love like Jesus:

not from a pedestal,

but from presence.

Reflection Questions

Where do you most need grace from your partner right now?

What situations trigger your impatience?

What old wound or past experience makes grace harder to give?

When has your partner extended grace to you in a way that deeply mattered?

What might change if you both offered just 10% more grace this week?

Homework for Chapter Five

1. The Grace Inventory

Each of you names one area where you need more grace — and one where you want to give more.

2. The Grace Pause

This week, when you feel annoyed, pause for five seconds and silently ask:

"What's the most gracious response right now?"

3. A Simple Blessing

"God, help us show grace to each other as freely as You show it to us."

Chapter Six

THE GIFT OF HONEST COMMUNICATION

If marriage had a number-one rule — above "don't weaponize the remote," above "don't eat the last slice unless you're prepared to negotiate peace treaties," above even "don't walk away when they're mid-sentence" — it would be this:

Tell the truth.

Kindly.

Consistently.

And preferably before resentment builds a guest house.

Healthy communication is not just a skill.

It's a gift you give each other.

And like any gift worth giving, it requires attention, intentionality, and sometimes deep breaths taken in the bathroom before re-entering the conversation.

Honest communication doesn't mean saying every thought that flies into your mind like a caffeinated moth. It means saying what is true — what actually matters — spoken in a way your partner can receive it without needing protective gear.

Put simply:

Honesty is the bridge.

Kindness is the traffic signal.

Love is the road.

And learning to drive that road together changes everything.

Why Honest Communication Is Harder Than It Sounds

There are a few reasons honesty in marriage can feel like walking a tightrope over a canyon filled with your partner's reactions:

1. Fear of hurting them

You love them. Hurting them feels like hurting yourself.

2. Fear of conflict

Some of us would rather fight a bear than have a difficult conversation.

3. Fear of being misunderstood

Nothing is worse than watching your sincere words turn into a misunderstanding tornado.

4. Fear of rejection

What if your truth pushes them away?

5. Old communication habits

If you grew up in a house where conflict was ignored, explosive, shame-based, or avoided, communication may feel like a risk rather than a normal part of life.

But here's the truth (ironically):

Honesty doesn't create distance.

Dishonesty does.

Honesty lets your partner see the real you.

Dishonesty forces them to guess.

And guessing games are fun for about five minutes at a baby shower, not for building a shared life.

Meet Trina and Miguel

Trina and Miguel were one of those couples who looked perfect from the outside — always smiling, always polite, always saying "We're good!" in that cheerful tone that makes you wonder if they've ever had a fight in their lives.

Behind closed doors, however, they struggled with one major issue: neither of them wanted to upset the other. Ever. Under any circumstances. Even slightly.

They tiptoed so carefully around each other's feelings that their emotional life started to resemble a house filled with bubble wrap and whispers.

When Trina felt overwhelmed by the household chores, she said nothing.

When Miguel felt lonely because Trina buried herself in work, he said nothing.

When resentments began forming like dust bunnies in the corners, they said... nothing.

Silence became their love language.

Unfortunately, silence is also the love language of distance, confusion, and feelings that gnaw quietly beneath the surface until they suddenly explode.

The explosion finally came in the form of an argument about — of course — something tiny. I believe it involved a grocery list, a misplaced onion, and two humans who had been swallowing their feelings for a little too long.

After the argument, they sat in exhausted honesty, staring at each other like two people who had just discovered the Earth was round.

Trina finally whispered, "I didn't want to burden you."

Miguel answered, "I didn't want you to think I was upset with you."

They laughed. Then cried. Then laughed again, because the whole thing was both tragic and deeply relatable.

And then they made a decision:

We tell the truth.

Gently, but consistently.

Things didn't magically become easy — but they became real.

And real is better than perfect.

Honesty + Kindness = Connection

Some people think honesty means brutal honesty.

Like:

"I'm just saying what I think,"

which is often code for

"I have not yet learned to season my truth with grace."

Then there's avoidant honesty, which is like whispering the truth into a pillow and hoping your partner hears it through osmosis.

What marriage needs is healthy honesty:

- grounded

- compassionate

- calm (or at least mostly calm)

- timely

- respectful

- clear

- When you combine honesty with kindness, something beautiful happens:

- Your partner feels safe.

- You feel understood.

And conversations stop feeling like minefields.

How to Say Hard Things Without Causing an Apocalypse

Here are some honest-but-kind phrases that save marriages on a regular basis:

"I'm not angry, but something's bothering me."

This softens the start-up.

"Can I share something without you thinking I'm attacking you?"

This invites collaboration.

"When you said/did _______, I felt _______."

Feelings, not accusations.

"Can we talk about this when we're both less emotional?"

A wise time-out is not avoidance; it's stewardship.

"I want us to understand each other, not win."

This shifts the goal from victory to connection.

"Help me understand what you meant."

Curiosity beats assumptions every time.

"This matters to me because..."

Vulnerability builds trust.

These are not scripts — just training wheels.

Use them until honesty feels natural, not performative.

Listening: The Other Half of Honesty

Being honest is only half the equation.

Listening is the other half — and sometimes, the harder half.

Because real listening requires:

staying quiet long enough to hear the whole truth

fighting the urge to prepare your comeback while they're talking

resisting the temptation to explain yourself too early

believing their feelings are real, even if they don't match your intent

remembering that understanding comes before resolution

Listening is an act of love.

It whispers, "Your experience matters as much as mine."

The moment your partner feels heard is the moment their defenses begin to soften.

Honesty Builds Safety

The more honestly you share with each other, the more emotionally safe your marriage becomes.

And emotional safety isn't soft or sentimental — it's strong.

It's the foundation that lets you bring:

- your fears

- your needs

- your insecurities

- your disappointments

- your dreams

- your hopes

- your messy thoughts

- your changing perspectives

into the relationship without worrying you'll be punished for them.

Honesty creates intimacy.

Dishonesty creates isolation.

The Beauty of Being Known Fully

There's a line in Scripture that says, "Perfect love casts out fear." (1 John 4:18)

Not perfect performance.

Not perfect communication.

Not perfect conflict resolution.

Perfect love.

When you practice honest communication, you are choosing intimacy over fear, clarity over confusion, and growth over stagnation.

You're saying,

"I trust you with the real me —

and I want the real you too."

That mutual exchange is holy ground.

It's where love becomes something deeper than romance —

it becomes companionship of the soul.

Reflection Questions

What makes honesty difficult for you in certain moments?

What kinds of truth do you tend to avoid sharing?

How do you respond when your partner tells you something hard?

How does it feel when you tell the truth and are met with kindness?

What is one small truth you want to practice sharing this week?

Homework for Chapter Six

1. The "Truth in Two Sentences" Exercise

Each partner shares one truth they've been holding back — but only in two sentences.

Short. Clear. Kind.

2. Listening Without Fixing

For one conversation this week, aim to listen without offering solutions.

Just presence.

3. A Simple Prayer

"God, help our honesty be gentle and our listening be generous."

Chapter Seven
Learning to Fight Fair

If there's one universal truth about marriage, it's this:

At some point, you're going to fight.

Not because you're incompatible.

Not because you chose the wrong person.

Not because you lack communication skills, spiritual maturity, or access to excellent burritos.

You're going to fight because you are two humans with different brains, different histories, different emotional wiring, and different instincts about everything from finances to the appropriate number of throw pillows a couch should have.

Fighting isn't a sign of failure.

It's a sign of closeness.

Only the people we love most have the power to trigger us so deeply.

The goal is not to avoid conflict.

The goal is to avoid damage.

That's what fighting fair is all about — learning to disagree in ways that protect the relationship, even when you don't feel particularly loving in the moment.

Conflict Doesn't Mean Something's Wrong

There's a myth — probably created by people who have been married for a total of eight minutes — that healthy relationships are conflict-free.

Nope.

Healthy relationships are repair-rich.

They fight.

They resolve.

They reconnect.

They grow.

Think of conflict like a storm.

Some storms are quick and cleansing.

Some are loud and dramatic.

Some require umbrellas and a warm blanket afterward.

But storms aren't the problem.

It's the foundation that matters.

A strong foundation can weather conflict.

A fragile one crumbles.

Learning to fight fair strengthens the foundation.

Meet Andrew and Felicity

Andrew and Felicity had two very different conflict styles, which made for a very exciting first year of marriage.

Felicity was a verbal processor — the kind of person who needs to talk everything out immediately, or her brain starts itching. When she was upset, it came out fast, fierce, and with the dramatic energy of a telenovela, complete with gestures.

Andrew, meanwhile, was a quiet processor. He needed time to collect his thoughts, check his emotions, and retreat into what he called "The Cave." (Not a literal cave — although he did consider buying a weighted blanket shaped like a rock.)

Their conflicts went like this:

Felicity: "We need to talk about this right now."

Andrew: "I need space so I don't say something I regret."

Felicity: "Space is abandonment!"

Andrew: "Talking right now is overwhelming!"

Both: frustrated noises

Neither person was wrong.

But they weren't fighting fair.

The breakthrough came one night when Andrew said, "I need you to trust my silence," and Felicity responded, "I need you to trust my urgency."

Two different needs.

Neither unreasonable.

Both holy.

Once they understood each other's conflict instincts, they made a plan:

Andrew would take a short break, not a disappearing act.

Felicity would let him retreat — but with a time limit.

They would always return to finish the conversation.

No sulking, no ice, no silent punishment.

That plan didn't make conflict easy,

but it made conflict safe.

And safety is everything.

The Rules of Fighting Fair

Here are the essentials — simple, human, deeply effective.

1. Stay on the issue, not the person

Don't bring up every fight you've ever had since 2009.

Don't stack grievances like firewood.

Stay with the moment at hand.

2. No mind-reading

If you're not a licensed telepath, don't assume intent.

Start with curiosity:

"Help me understand what happened."

3. No character assassination

"You always..."

"You never..."

"You're just like your mother..."

...these statements end marriages, not fights.

4. No silent treatment

Silence punishes.

Space heals.

5. Use "I" statements, not "You" grenades

"I felt hurt when..."

not

"You made me..."

6. Don't fight to win

If someone wins, the relationship loses.

7. Take breaks when needed

Breaks are not escape routes.

Breaks are buffers.

8. Assume good intentions

Most conflict isn't about malice.

It's about miscommunication, stress, fatigue, or fear.

9. Apologize quickly, sincerely, and without qualifiers

No "but."

No "if."

Just responsibility.

10. End with reconnection

Hold hands.

Hug.

Repeat what you appreciate about each other.

The end of a fight should bring you closer.

The Three Conflict Instincts

Most people lean toward one of these:

1. Pursuer

Wants to talk immediately.

Feels unsafe with silence.

Interprets withdrawal as rejection.

2. Withdrawer

Needs time to process.

Feels unsafe with intensity.

Interprets urgency as overwhelm.

3. The Internalizer

Doesn't lash out or retreat — just quietly absorbs everything until their emotional breaker flips.

Knowing your style (and your partner's) is half the battle.

The other half is offering grace for the differences.

Pursuers need patience.

Withdrawers need gentleness.

Internalizers need space to articulate feelings without pressure.

Avoiding the Four Horsemen

Psychologist John Gottman famously identified four behaviors that predict relationship doom with unsettling accuracy. Consider these the "Thou shalt not" commandments of marital conflict:

1. Criticism

Attacking your partner's character instead of the issue.

2. Contempt

Eye-rolling, sarcasm, mockery — relational poison.

3. Defensiveness

Turning every comment into a courtroom rebuttal.

4. Stonewalling

Shutting down emotionally and disappearing behind a wall.

The antidotes?

Gentle start-ups

Appreciation

Responsibility-taking

Healthy breaks

None of these are glamorous,

but they are incredibly effective.

Fighting Fair Means Fighting Together Against the Problem

Marriages fall apart when partners fight each other.

Marriages grow when partners fight side by side against the problem.

Imagine the problem as a third thing sitting on the table — something you and your partner turn toward together:

"How do we solve this?"

"What are we missing?"

"What would help us communicate better?"

Language matters.

Perspective matters.

Teamwork matters.

Because ultimately:

The *problem* is the problem.

Your partner is *not* the problem.

Conflict Can Be Holy

It sounds odd, but it's true:

Conflict can be a spiritual practice.

It's where your patience gets tested,

your compassion gets exercised,

your ego gets humbled,

your love gets refined,

and your grace gets stretched into new shapes.

Fighting fairly is one of the ways we imitate Christ —

not by avoiding hard truths,

but by speaking them with gentleness and receiving them with humility.

Conflict doesn't ruin relationships.

Avoidance does.

Contempt does.

Cruelty does.

But conflict handled with kindness?

That can build some of the strongest marriages on earth.

Reflection Questions

Which conflict instinct do you tend toward — pursuer, withdrawer, or internalizer?

Which tendencies in conflict frustrate your partner the most?

How did your family of origin handle conflict? How does that show up now?

What rule of fighting fair do you want to practice this week?

What helps you feel safe in conflict? What helps your partner?

Homework for Chapter Seven

1. The Conflict Styles Conversation

Each of you shares your instinctive style and one thing that helps you stay grounded during conflict.

2. Create a "Fair Fight Plan"

Agree on:

how to take breaks

how to reconnect

how to signal, "I need a pause"

how to return to the conversation

3. A Simple Prayer

"God, teach us to be gentle with each other, even in conflict."

Chapter Eight

THE LOST ART OF APOLOGIZING

You'd think apologizing would be simple. We learn to say "sorry" before we can tie our shoes. We say it when we bump into someone, when we interrupt, when we drop a fork, when we sneeze too loudly in public, and sometimes when we have absolutely nothing to apologize for ("Sorry, your plant died," as if we personally suffocated it).

But real apologizing?

The kind that heals?

The kind that restores connection in marriage?

That's practically an endangered art form.

Most of us were never taught how to apologize well. We either inherited apology habits from our families ("Say sorry right now or else") or picked them up from sitcoms where everyone forgives each other in 22 minutes with background laughter.

Marriage, however, calls for something deeper. Something honest. Something humble.

Something that actually repairs the moment.

Because here's a truth worth putting on a bumper sticker:

You can't be in a committed relationship

without occasionally stepping on each other's hearts.

And when that happens — as it inevitably will — you need a way back to each other.

That way back is an apology.

Not an excuse.

Not a justification.

Not an explanation disguised as understanding.

An apology.

When "Sorry" Isn't Really Sorry

We've all heard the non-apology apology:

"I'm sorry you feel that way."

Translation: "Your feelings are inconvenient for me."

Or:

"I'm sorry if I upset you."

Translation: "I'm not convinced I did anything wrong, but here's a participation trophy."

Then there's the always popular:

"I'm sorry, but..."

Anything before the "but" gets vaporized.

These formulas don't heal. They protect the ego at the expense of intimacy. They offer the illusion of repair without the substance of connection.

Real apologies?

Those are made of sturdier stuff.

Meet Evelyn and Jonah

Evelyn and Jonah were devoted, loving, thoughtful people. They were also unintentionally terrible at apologizing.

When Jonah forgot important dates (which he did often enough that Evelyn considered installing reminder alarms on his forehead), he would say, "I'm sorry, but you know how my brain works."

When Evelyn snapped under stress, she would say, "I'm sorry if you felt attacked," placing the entire burden on Jonah's feelings instead of her tone.

Neither meant harm.

But neither understood how their "apologies" were widening the emotional gap between them.

One night, after an argument that somehow escalated from laundry to childhood trauma in under twelve minutes, Jonah sat on the edge of the bed and said something profoundly vulnerable:

"I don't think I've ever learned how to apologize without defending myself."

Evelyn stared at him.

Then she whispered, "Me neither."

It was a holy moment — two imperfect people realizing they weren't bad at marriage; they were just under-equipped.

And grace rushed in.

What a Real Apology Sounds Like

A good apology has four simple elements:

1. Acknowledgment

Name what happened.

The real thing. Not the softened version.

2. Impact

Show you understand how it affected your partner.

3. Responsibility

Own your part without blame or excuses.

4. Commitment

Offer a plan — even a small one — to do better next time.

Put it all together and you get something like:

"I'm sorry I dismissed your concern earlier. I can see it hurt you and made you feel unheard. That wasn't fair. Next time I'll slow down and actually listen before responding."

Notice:

- It doesn't grovel.

- It doesn't dramatize.

- It doesn't self-blame.

- It simply takes responsibility.

That's the heartbeat of repair.

Why Apologizing Is So Hard

You'd think the difficulty would be in the words.

But really?

It's in the emotions underneath.

An apology requires vulnerability.

It requires stepping out from behind your ego and saying:

"I messed up, I see that, and our connection matters more to me than my pride."

That's scary. Even for emotionally mature grown-ups.

We fear an apology will become:

- a confession of incompetence

- a pass for our partner to be angry

- an imbalance of power

- an invitation for criticism

- a spotlight on our flaws

But none of that is true.

An apology doesn't make you weak. It makes you trustworthy.

It says, "Your heart matters to me more than looking perfect."

If that's not strength, what is?

Repair Attempts: The Everyday Apologies

Not every hurt requires a full four-step apology. Some wounds are small. Some conflicts are tiny. And sometimes what you really need isn't a speech — it's a repair attempt.

A repair attempt is a quick, quiet act of reconnection.

It might be:

- a hand on the back

- a soft "Hey... are we okay?"

- a gentle joke to break the tension

- a small act of service

- a hug

- a simple: "I'm sorry. That was my bad."

Repair attempts stop little cracks from becoming fractures.

They are the relational superglue.

Couples who repair quickly don't avoid conflict —

they just don't let conflict become corrosion.

Childhood Lessons (Good or Bad)

Most of us learned our apology style long before adulthood:

Some grew up in homes where apologies were forced and meaningless.

Some lived in households where no one ever apologized — ever.

Some learned to apologize for everything, even the weather.

Some learned apologies were dangerous because they invited shame.

These patterns don't vanish when we get married.

They follow us like emotional luggage.

The good news?

You can unpack.

Together.

A marriage full of grace is not one where both partners already know how to apologize — but one where both partners want to learn.

Timing Is Everything

Here's a truth that will save you years of frustration:

Even the best apology will backfire if delivered at the wrong moment.

If your partner is still emotionally activated, overwhelmed, raw, or flooded, your apology might feel like pressure, not healing.

Wait until their nervous system settles.

Wait until your defenses settle.

Then apologize.

You're not delaying healing — you're preserving it.

Letting Go of "Right"

One of the biggest barriers to apologizing?

Our obsession with being right.

We think apologizing means admitting defeat.

But marriage isn't a debate club.

There are no trophies for winning arguments.

Sometimes saying, "I'm sorry," is simply acknowledging:

"This relationship matters more than proving my point."

If both partners hold that posture,

peace blossoms.

Forgiveness Is Separate

Even the perfect apology doesn't guarantee immediate forgiveness.

Your partner gets to move at their pace.

An apology opens the door.

Forgiveness walks through it.

Respect the timing.

Honor the process.

Love them through it.

Reflection Questions

How were apologies handled in your family growing up?

Which part of apologizing feels hardest for you — acknowledgment, impact, responsibility, or commitment?

When has your partner apologized in a way that meant a lot to you?

What do you need from your partner during moments of repair?

What kind of apology helps you feel most safe?

Homework for Chapter Eight

1. Practice a Simple Four-Part Apology

Pick a small moment — tiny — and walk through the process.

2. Share Your Apology Styles

Talk openly about what helps and what doesn't.

3. Try One Repair Attempt This Week

A soft "Hey... I'm sorry about earlier" is enough to change the tone of a whole evening.

Chapter Nine

EMOTIONAL SAFETY: BUILDING A SANCTUARY TOGETHER

Every couple has that moment — sometimes early, sometimes years in — when they realize something quietly profound:

"I can be myself with you."

Not the polished self.

Not the polite self you bring to work or church or dinner with your in-laws.

Not the "I've-got-it-all-together" version of yourself you present to the world.

The real you.

The vulnerable you.

The one who feels things deeply, worries too much, gets overwhelmed, needs reassurance, whispers prayers, loses patience, cries at commercials, and occasionally eats cereal at midnight while standing in front of the fridge.

Emotional safety is the freedom to bring this full, unfiltered self into the relationship without fear.

It's the knowledge that your partner won't punish you, shame you, mock you, abandon you, or belittle your feelings.

It's the confidence that your inner world will be met with tenderness, not judgment.

In a world that often demands constant performance, emotional safety in marriage feels like stepping barefoot onto holy ground.

What Emotional Safety Looks Like (and What It Doesn't)

Emotional safety is not:

- perfect harmony

- never disagreeing

- never getting triggered

- never having bad days

- always saying the right thing

- always responding with Zen-like calm

Nope.

Emotional safety isn't the absence of conflict —

it's the presence of gentleness.

It looks like:

- soft eyes instead of sharp ones

- curiosity instead of assumptions

- pauses instead of explosions

- "Tell me more" instead of "That makes no sense"

- "I'm here" instead of "Calm down"

Emotional safety says,

"I can hold your feelings even when they're different from mine."

Meet Jasmine and Taylor

Jasmine and Taylor were opposites in all the classic ways. Jasmine was calm, measured, thoughtful — the emotional equivalent of a well-organized library. Taylor, on the other hand, felt emotions like a thunderstorm: loud, expressive, occasionally dramatic, and surprisingly refreshing.

When they first married, this difference felt cute.

Their friends even joked: "You're the perfect emotional thermostat!"

But when real stress hit — job transitions, health scares, aging parents — their differences became sources of tension.

Taylor would express everything loudly and immediately. Jasmine, overwhelmed, would retreat — not because she didn't care, but because her nervous system needed quiet to process.

This created an emotional loop of confusion:

Taylor felt abandoned.

Jasmine felt flooded.

Both felt misunderstood.

One day, after a tense argument that left them feeling bruised, they finally had the conversation that changed everything.

"I need space to think," Jasmine said quietly.

"I need connection when I'm hurting," Taylor said softly.

They stared at each other — surprised to discover that neither need was unreasonable.

And then came the breakthrough:

"What if we didn't see each other's reactions as threats,

but as needs?"

So they made a plan.

When Taylor was overwhelmed, Jasmine would sit nearby — not talking, but present.

When Jasmine was flooded, Taylor would soften her tone and slow down.

They created a sanctuary between them.

And slowly, the storm stopped feeling dangerous.

It started feeling like weather they could navigate together.

Why Emotional Safety Matters

You can have great communication skills, excellent conflict tools, beautiful date nights, shared values, and matching his-and-hers slippers...

but without emotional safety, none of it sticks.

Emotional safety creates:

1. Connection

You bond when you feel safe enough to be vulnerable.

2. Honesty

Truth only surfaces when it won't be punished.

3. Healing

Unhealed wounds need gentle environments.

4. Resilience

Couples who feel safe bounce back faster from conflict.

5. Passion

Nothing deepens intimacy — emotional or physical — like trust.

6. Growth

People grow when they feel supported, not criticized.

Emotional safety is the greenhouse where love thrives.

How Emotional Safety Gets Broken

Safety is fragile. It can be cracked by:

- sudden anger

- mockery

- dismissive comments

- unpredictable reactions

- emotional withdrawal

- sarcasm during vulnerable moments

- cold silence

- criticism disguised as "helpful advice"

- the infamous eye roll (the silent thunderclap of contempt)

These things don't break a marriage instantly.

But they do erode trust over time.

The good news?

Emotional safety can be rebuilt.

Not overnight.

Not through grand gestures.

But through small, steady practices of gentleness.

The Small Practices That Build Emotional Safety

Here's the good stuff — the practical things that transform relationships:

1. Validate First, Fix Later

When your partner opens up, start with:

"I hear you."

"That makes sense."

"I can see why you felt that way."

Solutions can come later.

Validation opens the door.

2. Lower Your Volume When Their Emotions Rise

Not just literal volume — emotional volume.

Gentleness calms storms faster than logic.

3. Stay Present, Even When It's Hard

You don't have to have the perfect response.

Sometimes all someone needs is:

"I'm here."

4. Ask What They Need

Not what you would want.

Not what you think they should want.

Ask:

"What would help right now?"

5. Own Your Tone

Tone communicates more than content.

You can say the right words in the wrong tone and still do damage.

6. Repair Quickly

"Hey, I was tense earlier. That's on me. Are we okay?"

Small repair attempts build big safety.

7. Listen Without Defending

This is the emotional equivalent of walking on water.

But once you practice it, your marriage transforms.

Seeing Each Other's Inner Worlds

One of the sweetest parts of emotional safety is learning your partner's internal landscape:

- what scares them

- what comforts them

- what overwhelms them

- what calms them

- what triggers old wounds

- what makes them feel cherished

- what helps them feel seen

This is sacred knowledge.

Handle it gently.

Your partner didn't reveal their heart so you could use it as ammunition.

They revealed it because they trust you.

Honor that trust.

The Spiritual Call to Safety

Throughout Scripture, we see God meeting people with gentleness:

Elijah, discouraged and afraid

Hagar, abandoned and unseen

Mary, confused and overwhelmed

Thomas, doubting and uncertain

Peter, ashamed after failure

God doesn't shame them.

God comforts them.

God listens.

God restores.

Emotional safety in marriage is one of the ways we reflect the heart of God —

creating a space where both people can come as they are,

not as they think they should be.

A safe marriage is a sanctuary —

not free of struggles,

but free of fear.

Reflection Questions

When do you feel most emotionally safe with your partner?

When do you feel least safe — and why?

What behaviors from your partner help you open up?

What behaviors from you help them feel protected?

What is one thing you both could do this week to increase emotional safety?

Homework for Chapter Nine

1. The Comfort Inventory

Each partner answers:

"What helps you feel safe when you're upset?"

Share your lists.

2. Practice a Soft Start-Up

Begin one conversation this week with gentleness:

"I want to share something, and I trust you with it."

3. A Simple Prayer

"God, make our home a refuge of kindness."

Chapter Ten

HOW TO TALK ABOUT THE HARD STUFF

Every couple has a list of conversations they avoid.

Not because they don't care, not because they're immature, not because they're incompatible — but because some topics feel like walking barefoot across emotional Legos.

The hard stuff might be:

- Money

- Boundaries with family

- Intimacy

- Mental health

- Spending habits

- Parenting styles

- Major life changes

- Hurt feelings

- Fears

- Old wounds

- Secret frustrations

- That one habit your partner has that makes you pray for patience and/or divine intervention

Hard conversations aren't hard because you're doing marriage wrong.

They're hard because you're talking about things that matter.

No one has a difficult conversation about something they don't care about.

The difficulty itself is proof of love.

Avoidance: The Silent Marriage Killer

Most couples don't mean to avoid hard conversations — they just tell themselves:

"We'll talk about it later."

"We don't have time right now."

"It'll blow over."

"It's not worth fighting about."

"Let me just wait until I'm in a better mood, a better place, or a better version of myself."

But avoidance doesn't dissolve tension.

It stores it — like leftovers shoved in the back of the fridge until someone opens the door and screams, "What is that smell?"

Avoided conversations eventually leak out sideways —

in short tempers, in distance, in passive-aggressive comments, in apathy, in assumptions, in sleepless nights spent staring at the ceiling thinking,

"Okay but seriously... are we going to talk about this or not?"

Avoidance doesn't preserve peace.

It delays clarity.

Meet Noah and Elena

Noah and Elena had one of those seemingly peaceful marriages — the kind where friends said, "They never fight. They must be soulmates." And while yes, they adored each other... there was a reason they never fought:

They never talked about anything hard.

Noah didn't want to burden Elena with work stress.

Elena didn't want to burden Noah with financial worries.

They tiptoed around the edges of every problem like two people trying not to wake a sleeping cat — which is adorable until you realize the cat is actually a tiger.

The "big conversation" finally hit one Friday evening after Noah snapped about a late Amazon package. (It always starts with something ridiculous.) Suddenly, years of unspoken fears came rushing out — not perfectly, not calmly, but truthfully.

They talked for hours.

There were tears.

There were long silences.

There were moments of "I didn't know you felt that way."

And afterward, they both said the same thing:

"Why didn't we talk like this sooner?"

Hard conversations broke their silence — and rebuilt their marriage.

Why Hard Conversations Feel Scary

Talking about hard things triggers old fears:

"What if I start a fight?"

"What if they get angry?"

"What if they think I'm criticizing them?"

"What if I look needy?"

"What if I don't say it right?"

"What if this changes everything?"

But here's the truth your marriage needs:

The only thing harder than hard conversations is living with the distance created by avoiding them.

You're not protecting the relationship by staying silent.

You're starving it.

The Art of Gentle Truth

Hard conversations don't have to be explosions.

They can be soft, slow, and kind.

Imagine them like approaching a skittish animal — calm body language, soft voice, lots of patience.

Here's how to talk about hard things without setting off emotional fireworks:

1. Choose timing wisely

Don't start a deep conversation when:

- someone is exhausted

- someone is stressed

- someone is hungry

- someone is watching a show

- someone is in the middle of concentrating

- someone is actively holding a chainsaw (hopefully rare)

Try:

"Hey, could we talk about something important later? I want to do it gently."

This sets the tone.

2. Start softly

Harsh beginnings guarantee harsh endings.

Try:

"I love you, and I want us to understand each other better."

or

"There's something on my heart I'd like to share."

3. Be honest AND kind

Not brutal honesty.

Not passive honesty.

Just clear, compassionate honesty.

4. Stay on one topic

Don't start with finances and end with "and another thing!"

One issue at a time.

Your marriage is not a courtroom deposition.

5. Use "I feel" statements

Not "You always" or "You never."

Those shut down listening.

Try:

"I feel worried when..."

"I feel disconnected when..."

"I feel overwhelmed by..."

6. Ask questions instead of assuming

"Help me understand."

"What were you feeling?"

"What would help?"

Curiosity pulls you together.

7. Take breaks when needed

If emotions spike, pause.

Not forever — just enough to breathe.

8. Reconnect when it's over

Hold hands.

Hug.

Pray.

Affirm.

Make sure the conversation ends in closeness, not tension.

The Gift of Being Heard

Hard conversations go wrong when both partners try to talk at the same time — emotionally or literally.

The real magic happens when one person speaks and the other listens as if the words matter.

Because they do.

Listening transforms hard conversations from battles into bridges.

When your partner feels heard:

- their defenses lower

- their fear softens

- their trust deepens

- their heart opens

Listening doesn't mean you agree with everything.

It means you care enough to understand before responding.

That alone can save marriages.

What Hard Conversations Can Reveal

If you approach them with gentleness, honesty, and curiosity, hard conversations can be incredibly life-giving. They reveal:

- unmet needs

- unspoken fears

- old wounds

- unaddressed patterns

- hopes you didn't know your partner carried

- ways you can love each other more intentionally

Hard conversations aren't just about solving problems.

They're about revealing parts of each other you might not have noticed.

They deepen love because they deepen understanding.

Putting the Gospel Into Practice

In Scripture, God never avoids the hard stuff.

Jesus talks about truth constantly — but always with compassion.

He speaks truth that heals, truth that restores, truth that draws people closer.

Hard conversations in marriage are a chance to imitate this kind of love —

the kind that's honest without being harsh,

courageous without being cruel,

truthful without being terrifying.

This is relational discipleship.

This is spiritual intimacy.

This is love in motion.

Reflection Questions

What hard conversation have you been avoiding, and why?

What fears come up for you when facing difficult topics?

How do you prefer hard conversations to begin?

When has a hard conversation actually brought you closer?

What would support look like for you during a difficult talk?

Homework for Chapter Ten

1. Choose One "Hard Thing" and Name It

Not to fix it yet — just to bring it into the light.

2. The "Gentle Start-Up" Practice

Begin a tough conversation with kindness this week.

3. A Simple Prayer

"God, give us courage to speak truth and gentleness to hear it."

Chapter Eleven

PRAYING TOGETHER (WITHOUT IT FEELING WEIRD)

If there is one spiritual practice everybody assumes married couples are naturally good at, it's praying together. People talk about it as if it's as simple as brushing your teeth or remembering your anniversary (which, let's be honest, isn't always simple either).

But the truth?

Even couples who have been in church their entire lives often find praying together awkward... intimidating... or just plain weird.

Why?

Because prayer is vulnerable.

It's intimate.

It reveals what's going on inside your heart.

It exposes fears, hopes, doubts, gratitude, insecurities, regrets, and dreams.

Praying together is like opening your soul in front of someone and saying,

"Here. This is me. The whole me."

And that's beautiful —

but also a little terrifying.

If praying together feels unnatural or clumsy, congratulations:

You are normal.

Let's take the pressure off right from the start.

Why Praying Together Often Feels Awkward

There are a few reasons couples struggle with shared prayer, even when they deeply love God and each other:

1. Fear of sounding "unspiritual"

We imagine our prayers need to sound poetic or profound, like we're auditioning for the role of Heavenly Narrator.

2. Fear of being judged

"What if my partner thinks my prayer is silly... or too emotional... or not emotional enough?"

3. Different prayer backgrounds

One partner grew up praying spontaneously.

The other grew up saying scripted prayers. One prays long prayers. The other prays short ones.

One prays like a poet.

The other prays like they're leaving a voicemail.

4. Vulnerability hangover

Praying reveals your insides.

Not everyone is ready to pour out their soul at 7:15 p.m. on a Tuesday.

5. Pressure

Some couples try too hard.

They think joint prayer means a 40-minute devotional with hand-holding and candlelight, instead of something simple, natural, and human.

But praying together doesn't have to be dramatic.

It doesn't have to be formal.

It doesn't have to be long.

It just has to be real.

Meet Chris and Daniel

Chris and Daniel had been together for four years when they admitted a slightly embarrassing truth:

They had no idea how to pray together.

Daniel grew up in a church where people prayed like they were verbally wrestling angels. Loud, passionate, emotional.

Chris grew up in quiet liturgical spaces where prayer happened in whispers, readings, and long stretches of silence.

Their first attempt at praying together was... let's call it "a learning experience."

Chris bowed his head and waited.

Daniel bowed his head and waited.

They both waited.

They waited long enough for their dog to assume something was wrong.

Finally Daniel peeked and whispered,

"Are you going to start?"

Chris whispered back,

"I thought you were going to start."

They laughed until they were crying.

And in that moment of awkward honesty... something holy happened.

Laughter broke the fear.

Grace entered the room.

And they found a way forward — not through perfection, but through authenticity.

What Praying Together Can Create

When couples pray together — awkwardly or beautifully or somewhere in between — something shifts.

Prayer builds:

1. Emotional Intimacy

You hear each other's hearts in ways normal conversation rarely reveals.

2. Spiritual Connection

You remember that you're not just partners — you're pilgrims walking the same sacred road.

3. Protection Against Resentment

It's hard to stay bitter toward someone you're holding hands with while whispering, "God, help us love each other well."

4. Clarity

Prayer slows everything down.

It helps you see what matters and what doesn't.

5. Humility

When you pray together, you remind yourselves that you don't have to carry everything alone.

Prayer doesn't solve every problem.

But it tills the soil of the heart so solutions can grow.

Start Small, Start Simple

Here's the secret to praying together without making it weird:

Pray as yourselves.

Not as who you think you should be.

Not as who your former pastor was.

Not as the couple on Instagram with matching Bibles and latte art.

Just... you.

Try starting with something tiny:

"God, thank you for today."

Ten seconds. No pressure.

"Help us be patient with each other this week."

One sentence.

"Be with us in the things we're worried about."

Easy, honest, human.

This is prayer.

This counts.

Jesus never said, "Blessed are the couples who pray dramatically."

He said, "Blessed are the pure in heart."

Purity of heart is simplicity.

And simplicity builds connection.

Ways to Pray Together (That Don't Feel Forced)

Here are gentle, non-intimidating approaches:

1. Hold hands for ten seconds and pray silently.

Let God hear the words you're not ready to say aloud.

2. One person says one line. The other adds one line.

Short, soft, responsive.

3. Write short prayers in a shared journal.

Praying doesn't have to be verbal.

4. Use Scripture as a starting point.

"Love is patient, love is kind... God help us practice this today."

5. Pray while you're walking the dog.

Movement lowers pressure.

6. Pray blessings over each other.

"I bless you with peace this week."

"I bless your work day tomorrow."

"I bless your heart to feel safe and loved."

7. Pray for something simple together.

Someone in your life who needs encouragement.

A decision you're facing.

A fear one of you is carrying.

A gratitude you want to mark.

Prayer doesn't need candles, Gregorian chant, or early-morning devotionals with herbal tea (though if that's your thing — go forth and chant).

Prayer needs presence.

It needs openness.

It needs willingness.

And willingness is enough.

The Spiritual Vulnerability of Letting Yourself Be Seen

One of the sweetest outcomes of praying together is that you start to see your partner not just as your spouse or your companion — but as a soul.

You hear their fears:

"God, help me not worry so much."

You hear their love for you:

"Thank you for my partner."

You hear their hopes:

"Guide us."

You hear their tenderness:

"Keep them safe today."

Prayer reveals what the heart holds.

Sometimes it reveals fears you didn't know your partner had.

Sometimes it reveals gratitude you desperately needed to hear.

It's emotional exposure...

and emotional exposure builds intimacy.

When Prayer Feels Lopsided

Sometimes one partner feels more confident praying than the other.

That's okay.

Prayer is not a competition.

What matters is gentleness:

Don't correct each other's prayers.

Don't critique the wording.

Don't treat prayer like a performance.

Don't shame hesitation.

If your partner is shy or uncertain, treasure that vulnerability.

Hesitancy often means the moment matters to them.

Honor it.

When Prayer Feels Dry

Yes, even spiritual practices hit dry spells.

Sometimes one or both of you won't feel like praying.

Sometimes life gets heavy and the words won't come.

When that happens, try:

simple gratitude

silence together

reading a Psalm aloud

lighting a candle and sitting quietly

saying, "God, meet us here"

God does not require eloquence.

God requires honesty.

And honest silence is still prayer.

Reflection Questions

What emotions come up for you when you think about praying together?

What prayer habits did you learn growing up (good or bad)?

What type of prayer makes you feel safe?

How would you like to invite God into your relationship in this season?

What simple prayer could you offer together today?

Homework for Chapter Eleven

1. The 20-Second Prayer

Hold hands.

Close your eyes.

One of you says a single sentence.

Then switch.

Easy. Gentle. No pressure.

2. The Bedtime Blessing

Each night this week, say one blessing over your partner.

Just one.

3. A Simple Prayer

"God, knit our hearts together in love."

Chapter Twelve

THE POWER OF GRATITUDE IN MARRIAGE

If there's one spiritual practice that can quietly transform a marriage without requiring money, therapy, dramatic breakthroughs, or even leaving the couch, it's gratitude.

Gratitude is deceptively powerful — the kind of power that doesn't shout. It whispers. It whispers hope. It whispers acknowledgment. It whispers, "I see you," which, by the way, is one of the deepest needs every human carries.

Most marriages aren't destroyed by big, catastrophic failures.

Most crumble under the slow erosion of feeling unseen, unappreciated, or taken for granted.

Which means the antidote is surprisingly simple:

Notice your partner.

Name what you see.

Say thank you.

It's small, yes — but small practices create big transformations.

The Science (and Spirituality) of Gratitude

Psychologists have done all the studies: couples who regularly express gratitude have stronger emotional bonds, more satisfying communication, and better conflict recovery.

But long before psychology departments funded those studies, Scripture had already been saying the same thing:

"Give thanks in all circumstances."

"Encourage one another and build each other up."

"Love does not forget the good."

Gratitude is woven into the spiritual rhythm of Christianity — but it also happens to be one of the most practical habits for marriage.

Gratitude:

- softens resentment

- builds goodwill

- rewires the brain toward optimism

- increases affection

- deepens connection

- reminds you why you chose each other

It's basically miracle glue.

Divine duct tape.

Holy superpower gel.

Use generously.

Meet Brianna and Marcus

Brianna and Marcus loved each other deeply — no question. But after twelve years of marriage, they had fallen into what therapists call "functional partnership mode."

They were great teammates.

Efficient.

Responsible.

Good parents.

Competent adults.

But somewhere along the way, affection slipped.

Laughter got quieter.

And gratitude?

Well... let's just say it was implied, not spoken.

(Which is code for: it wasn't spoken.)

One night, after an exceptionally exhausting week, Marcus collapsed on the couch while Brianna was finishing dishes. Without looking up, she said, "I do everything around here."

Marcus sat up, startled.

Everything?

He wanted to argue — his brain had a PowerPoint ready — but something stopped him.

Maybe it was the weariness in her voice.

Maybe it was the fact that, deep down, he really hadn't thanked her for anything in a very long time.

So instead of defending himself, he walked into the kitchen, placed his hands on her shoulders, and said softly:

"I don't thank you enough. And I'm sorry. I really mean that."

She froze.

Not out of shock — okay, maybe a little shock — but out of relief.

Because she didn't actually want an argument.

She wanted acknowledgment.

That moment became a turning point.

They didn't overhaul their entire marriage in one night.

They just started saying "thank you" again.

To their surprise, gratitude became contagious.

The more they expressed it, the easier it became.

The easier it became, the more connected they felt.

The more connected they felt, the more natural their affection became.

It didn't solve everything.

But it softened everything.

Why Gratitude Feels So Hard Sometimes

You'd think gratitude would be easy.

But often, it's not — especially when life gets crowded.

Gratitude gets buried under:

- stress

- fatigue

- unmet expectations

- busyness

- unspoken disappointments

- familiarity

- mental load

- emotional load

- laundry (metaphorically and literally)

Sometimes the person who means the most to us becomes the person we thank the least — not because they're unworthy, but because they're constant. They're there every day. Doing what they do. Holding life together.

And familiarity breeds blindness.

Which means gratitude must be intentional — not accidental.

Seeing the Good (Even When You're Irritated)

Here's a surprising truth:

You can be annoyed by someone and still be grateful for them.

These two feelings are not mutually exclusive.

They coexist all the time in long-term relationships.

Gratitude doesn't require:

- a perfect partner

- a conflict-free season

- or a romantic mood

It just requires attention.

When irritation is high, gratitude gently taps you on the shoulder and says:

"Hey... remember the whole picture. Not just this moment."

Gratitude shifts perspective.

Not by denying frustration,

but by balancing it with reality.

Practical Ways to Build a Culture of Gratitude

Let's get tangible. Here are simple, non-cheesy ways to weave gratitude into your daily rhythm:

1. "Thank you for…"

Just one sentence. Daily.

"Thank you for making coffee."

"Thank you for checking on me."

"Thank you for folding laundry."

"Thank you for loving me."

2. The Two-Minute Gratitude Ritual

Sit together for two minutes at the end of the day.

Each person names one thing the other did that day that mattered.

3. The Gratitude Text

A spontaneous message:

"Thinking of you. You're wonderful."

It hits harder than you think.

4. The List

Once a month, write down five things you appreciate about your partner.

Swap lists.

5. Speak gratitude in front of others

You want to watch your partner glow?

Compliment them publicly.

(Not in a performative way — just authentically.)

6. Gratitude during conflict

"Yes, we're frustrated... but I'm still grateful for you."

Conflict changes tone immediately.

7. Gratitude for effort, not outcome

"I appreciate the effort you made,"

even if the effort didn't turn out perfect.

Effort is intimacy.

Notice it.

When Gratitude Reveals Something Missing

Sometimes gratitude exposes an uncomfortable truth:

"I want to be grateful...

but I don't know what to be grateful for right now."

If you feel this way, that's not a failure.

It's a signal.

It might mean:

- you're exhausted

- you're burned out

- you're carrying resentment

- you miss feeling seen

- you're overwhelmed

- something needs to be talked about

- healing is needed

Gratitude can't grow where connection is numb —

but it can revive connection once conversation begins.

Sometimes the most sacred thing you can say is:

"I want to get back to a place of gratitude. Can we talk?"

That honesty is gratitude in seed form.

Spiritual Gratitude: The Holiness of Seeing the Gift

Theologically speaking, gratitude is a form of worship.

It's a recognition that all good things come from God... including the person sitting across from you at the breakfast table, hair sticking up in fifteen directions.

When you say,

"Thank you for being you,"

you're echoing God's heart.

Gratitude is holiness in ordinary clothes.

It is prayer disguised as appreciation.

It is love wearing work boots.

And marriages need that kind of holiness — quiet, grounding, daily holiness.

Reflection Questions

What is something your partner does consistently that you rarely thank them for?

What makes expressing gratitude hard for you at times?

How did your family express (or not express) appreciation when you were growing up?

What's one form of gratitude that would make you feel especially loved?

What's one thing you can thank your partner for today?

Homework for Chapter Twelve

1. The Daily Thank-You

Every day this week, tell your partner one specific thing you're grateful for.

2. The "Unexpected Gratitude" Note

Leave a brief note somewhere they'll find it:

a lunch bag, dashboard, pillow, coffee mug, phone screen, or coat pocket.

3. A Simple Prayer

"God, open our eyes to the gifts we already have."

Chapter Thirteen

KEEPING ROMANCE ALIVE (WITHOUT FEELING LIKE YOU'RE FORCING IT)

Somewhere out there — probably on a beach, holding hands under a sunset that looks suspiciously Photoshopped — is a couple who claims their romance has never faded. They say they keep the spark alive effortlessly. No awkwardness. No dry seasons. No mismatched desires, schedules, or energy levels.

I'm happy for them.

Truly.

But the rest of us are out here living in the real world — where romance takes effort, timing, creativity, and sometimes a nap.

The truth is:

Romance isn't something you "have."

It's something you *create* — together — over and over again.

It doesn't have to be grand or dramatic.

It doesn't have to look like Instagram.

It doesn't have to feel like a movie soundtrack is playing in the background (although if that happens naturally, embrace it).

Romance simply means making each other feel chosen... again.

The Myth of "Effortless Romance"

There's a persistent myth — powered by fairy tales, rom-coms, and Hallmark movies filmed in suspiciously charming small towns — that romance should always feel natural.

But natural is unpredictable.

Natural has bad days.

Natural gets tired.

Natural forgets anniversaries, loses track of time, and occasionally falls asleep during date night.

Real romance is intentional.

That's not unspiritual or unsexy —

it's mature.

It's grounded.

It's sustainable.

Most beautifully, it's reachable for every couple.

Meet Carla and Joseph

Carla and Joseph had been married eight years when they realized something:

their romance hadn't disappeared — it had just gone to sleep somewhere under a pile of laundry.

Life had gotten full:

work

kids

pets

busy schedules

decreasing energy

and the shocking discovery that exhaustion arrives earlier in the evening every decade.

They loved each other. Deeply.

But their romantic life had drifted into "functional roommate mode."

One night, while sitting on the couch eating frozen pizza and watching a documentary about penguins, Carla sighed and said,

"Remember when we used to flirt?"

Joseph laughed — not because it was funny, but because it was painfully accurate.

So they made a small, simple pact:

One intentional moment of romance per day.

No pressure.

No performance.

Just one moment.

A flirty text.

A hand on the waist in the kitchen.

A long hug.

A whispered compliment.

A gentle kiss before work.

Lighting a candle during dinner.

Turning off phones after 8 p.m.

Trying again tomorrow if today's effort flopped.

Within a month, the spark wasn't simply back —

it was deeper, warmer, more mature, and more meaningful than before.

Not because they "reignited passion"...

but because they chose each other in small, daily ways.

Romance didn't return on its own.

They invited it.

Why Romance Fades (Even in Strong Relationships)

Romance fades because life grows.

And growing life takes space.

Romance gets crowded out by:

- responsibilities

- stress

- fatigue

- financial worries

- illness

- parenting

- mental load

- emotional load

- routines

- technology

- comfort (yes, even comfort can smother romance)

It's not moral failure.

It's not lack of love.

It's not incompatibility.

It's simply physics: if nothing intentional is added, the romantic cup evaporates slowly.

Romance fades naturally.

Reconnection happens deliberately.

The Three Kinds of Romance Every Couple Needs

Romance isn't just candlelight and physical affection.

It has layers — like relational lasagna.

1. Everyday Romance

Gentle moments of affection that say,

"I still choose you."

Examples:

- a lingering touch

- a playful comment

- holding hands

- looking at each other a little too long

- warming their coffee mug before you bring it to them

Everyday romance is the glue.

2. Intentional Romance

Things you plan because your partner matters.

Examples:

- date nights

- small surprises

- cooking a nice meal

- a thoughtful card

- planning an outing

Intentional romance is the spark.

3. Deep Romance

Moments that nourish the soul.

Examples:

- honest conversations

- shared dreams

- praying together

- comforting each other

- being vulnerable

- long hugs where breathing syncs

Deep romance is the anchor.

A healthy relationship needs all three —

not constantly, not perfectly,

but consistently over time.

The Romance Languages Beyond Love Languages

Yes, love languages matter — words, touch, gifts, time, acts of service.

But romance has its own set of languages:

1. Attentiveness

"I noticed this about you..."

2. Mystery

A little surprise goes a long way.

3. Playfulness

Laughing together can be more romantic than roses.

4. Initiative

Romance feels different when someone takes the lead.

5. Presence

Undistracted time — even five minutes — is pure gold.

6. Tenderness

Soft eyes.

Soft hands.

Soft tone.

It's irresistible.

7. Admiration

Letting your partner know you still find them captivating — inside and out.

You don't need all of these every day.

But sprinkling them over time?

That's romance that lasts.

The Sacred Role of Desire

Let's talk gently about desire.

Desire isn't just physical — it's emotional, spiritual, intellectual, relational.

But desire also fluctuates.

Seasons of low desire don't mean your love is failing — it means you're human.

Romance can still thrive in seasons of low physical energy or low libido when couples stay emotionally close, tender, playful, and communicative.

Romance is the broader landscape.

Physical intimacy is one beautiful part of it — not the whole story.

When couples stay connected emotionally, physical closeness becomes easier to reengage naturally.

What Romance Looks Like in Real Life

Let's demystify romance.

Here's what it looks like in the real world:

- slow dancing in the kitchen

- grocery store hand-holding

- taking a drive together

- flirty glances

- private jokes

- scarves shared in cold weather

- forehead kisses

- making their coffee just the way they like it

- massaging their shoulders while they vent

- choosing to sit next to them instead of across the room

- sending a playlist you made just for them

- lighting a candle during dinner on a random Tuesday

- taking a walk after dinner

- whispering "I'm glad you're mine" before bed

Romance isn't fancy.

It's presence plus intention.

Reflection Questions

When did you feel most romantically connected to your partner in the past month?

What kind of romance do you miss, and why?

What kinds of romantic gestures feel most meaningful to you?

What do you think your partner finds romantic that you haven't done lately?

What small act of romance could you offer today?

Homework for Chapter Thirteen

1. The One-Moment-a-Day Practice

Start small.

One romantic action per day — any size, any style.

2. Create a Tiny Romance Plan

Each partner writes down five romantic gestures they'd love.

Share your lists.

3. A Simple Prayer

"God, help our love be tender, playful, and renewed in spirit."

Chapter Fourteen

LEARNING TO REST TOGETHER

One of the most surprising discoveries couples make — usually sometime between the thrill of early romance and the long, steady rhythm of building a life — is that rest does not come naturally to everyone. In fact, for many couples, rest becomes one of the first things to erode when life gets busy. Work expands, responsibilities multiply, calendars fill, exhaustion sets in, and rest becomes something you "get around to" someday, which is usually code for "never."

And yet, learning to rest together is one of the most life-giving practices a couple can cultivate. Not just physical rest, though that matters. Emotional rest. Mental rest. Relational rest — the kind where you can simply be with each other without accomplishing anything, solving anything, or performing anything.

Rest is not laziness. It is a spiritual discipline wrapped in human necessity. It softens the edges, quiets the noise, and makes room for tenderness. Without rest, even the most loving couples start running on fumes. With it, marriages become gentler places, able to absorb stress and conflict more gracefully.

Rest is what reconnects you to yourself and to each other.

Why Rest Is Harder Than It Sounds

Many of us grew up in families or cultures where rest was seen as a luxury or an indulgence rather than a part of spiritual well-being. Some couples carry the unspoken belief that love is proven through productivity — through doing, achieving, fixing, providing, managing. Others simply get swept into the demands of life and forget to slow down.

Then there are the personality dynamics. One partner may recharge through quiet stillness while the other feels most rested when they're active and outside. One wants to nap on the couch with a blanket and a movie; the other feels restored by hiking, swimming, or exploring new places. One prefers an afternoon of silence; the other draws energy from music, conversation, and movement.

Learning to rest together doesn't mean you suddenly share the same rhythms. It simply means you make room for each other's ways of slowing down, and you find a few shared rhythms that nourish you both.

Different styles aren't obstacles. They're invitations.

Meet Hannah and Luke

Hannah and Luke had been married for six years when they realized their lives were full but their souls were tired. Luke worked long hours at a job he loved but that demanded constant emotional output. Hannah managed the household with an admirable blend of efficiency and exhaustion.

They weren't fighting.

They weren't unhappy.

They were simply running on empty.

One Saturday, after a week that felt like a month, Luke suggested they drive out to a nearby lake and spend the afternoon doing "absolutely nothing." Hannah hesitated — she had laundry to do, groceries to get, emails to answer, tasks to finish, responsibilities waiting. But something in her said yes. It wasn't a loud yes. It was more of a whispered permission slip.

They packed a blanket and some snacks, drove out to the lake, and stretched out under a wide blue sky. Luke dozed off within minutes. Hannah watched the ripples on the water, then finally exhaled — the kind of long, slow exhale that only comes when your soul remembers what peace feels like.

They didn't talk much that afternoon. They didn't plan anything. They didn't solve anything. But when they drove home, both felt lighter — not because the to-do list was done, but because their hearts had opened up again.

That day changed something. It wasn't a dramatic moment, just a quiet one. But it taught them that rest could be something they practiced together, not something they stumbled into by accident.

The Spiritual Practice of Shared Rest

Scripture paints rest as holy ground. The Sabbath wasn't given as a rule to restrict people; it was given as a gift to free them. Jesus consistently stepped away from crowds, noise, expectations, and responsibilities — not because he didn't care, but because he did. Rest was part of his rhythm of love.

In marriage, shared rest becomes a form of worship. It honors the gift of life. It honors the image of God in you and in your partner. It honors the fact that relationships flourish not only through effort but through stillness.

Rest says:

"We matter.

Our connection matters.

Our well-being matters.

And we don't have to earn permission to stop for a moment."

When couples slow down together, something quiet but powerful happens. Anxiety softens. Affection grows. Conversations become more relaxed. You laugh more easily. You touch more naturally. You remember the gentler parts of each other that get buried under stress.

Rest clears the spiritual clutter.

Finding Your Shared Rhythm

Every couple has their own blend of rest, and it rarely looks like anyone else's. Some couples reconnect by curling up on the couch with a blanket and a good series to watch. Others feel restored by long walks, by gardening, by playing a board game, or by sitting in a coffee shop reading quietly side by side. Some find rest in prayer or meditation; others in a slow dinner together without distractions.

The key is not to imitate someone else's rhythm but to learn your own.

Ask each other:

- What kind of rest actually restores you?

- What kind of rest leaves you feeling drained or restless?

- What activities calm your mind?

- What helps your body relax?

- What helps your soul breathe more deeply?

You might discover surprising things.

One partner may feel rested after decluttering a room.

The other may feel rested after doing absolutely nothing at all.

Both are valid. Both can coexist.

The beauty of shared rest is not uniformity — it's gentleness.

Rest as Connection, Not Escape

Some people mistake rest for numbing out — scrolling endlessly, zoning out until hours pass, or retreating into habits that don't actually restore. There's a difference between escape and restoration. Escape helps you avoid feelings; rest helps you feel grounded enough to face them.

Shared rest is not about checking out from each other.

It's about checking in with yourselves, together.

It builds connection in a different way than conversation or romance or problem-solving. It builds the kind of connection that comes when you're simply present with each other in a moment of calm, unhurried, unpressured being.

Think of it this way:

Talking connects your minds.

Affection connects your bodies.

Rest connects your souls.

When Rest Exposes Unspoken Tension

Rest can bring clarity.

And sometimes that clarity brings up things you've been avoiding.

Slowing down quiets the noise that normally distracts you from what's happening internally. If you find yourselves feeling anxious, irritable, or uncomfortable when you try to rest, it might be a sign that something needs to be named, not ignored. That doesn't make rest wrong — it makes it revealing.

Rest can gently uncover:

- simmering resentment

- unspoken fears

- unmet needs

- fatigue you've been powering through

- loneliness even inside a partnership

If rest reveals something tender, you can treat that revelation as an invitation to talk — softly, respectfully, without rush.

Sometimes the most healing conversations happen when you're relaxed enough to speak without defensiveness.

Small, Simple Ways to Rest Together

Here are some gentle, everyday practices that help cultivate shared rest:

- Sit together with your morning coffee without screens.

- Take a slow walk after dinner, even ten minutes.

- Listen to music together and let the moment breathe.

- Watch a sunset or sit outside as the light changes.

- Share a quiet meal, focusing on taste rather than efficiency.

- Give yourselves permission for a Sunday afternoon nap.

- Read side by side — same book or different ones.

- Light a candle and sit together in silence for five minutes.

- Hold hands and breathe slowly until your bodies relax.

- Rest doesn't have to be dramatic. The simplest moments are often the most healing.

Reflection Questions

What kind of rest restores you the most — physical, emotional, mental, or spiritual?

What does shared rest look like in your relationship right now?

When do you feel most calm with your partner?

Are there any obstacles (internal or external) that make rest difficult for you?

What small change could you make this week to create more shared rest?

Homework for Chapter Fourteen

1. Choose a Shared Rest Activity

Pick one simple, restorative activity and do it together this week — no multitasking, no rushing.

2. Talk About Rest Styles

Share with each other two things that help you feel rested and two things that drain you.

3. A Simple Prayer

"God, teach us the grace of slowing down together."

Chapter Fifteen

UNTANGLING EXPECTATIONS

Every couple enters marriage carrying an invisible backpack full of expectations. Most of the time we don't even know what's in it until we trip over something and wonder why it hurt so much. Expectations about communication, roles, holidays, affection, money, tidiness, emotional responses, social life, spirituality, intimacy — the list goes on. Some expectations are spoken. Most aren't.

And here's the thing about expectations: they are powerful.

Quietly powerful.

Sometimes lovingly powerful.

Sometimes explosively powerful.

They shape how we interpret our partner's actions.

They influence how we react when something feels wrong.

They determine what we see as normal, thoughtful, inconsiderate, generous, or disappointing.

The problem is not that we have expectations — every human being does. The problem is when we assume our expectations are universal, obvious, or "just common sense."

Nothing is universal in marriage.

Common sense is not always common.

And "obvious" usually isn't.

Untangling expectations isn't about lowering standards or settling for less. It's about gaining clarity, learning what each other needs, and understanding that two good people can still have wildly different assumptions about what love should look like.

The Most Dangerous Expectations Are the Unspoken Ones

Disappointment often comes from expectations we never communicated. We assume our partner will naturally understand:

- how we want to be comforted

- what holidays should look like

- how finances should be handled

- what "helping around the house" means

- how much affection we need

- how often we want to connect

- when we need space

- how we feel loved

- how decisions should be made

- what "being on time" means

- how chores should be divided

- how conflict should be handled

We assume our partner will just know.

Because if they really loved us, they would get it.

Right?

Not exactly.

Love makes people care.

It doesn't make them psychic.

Meet Janelle and Omar

Janelle and Omar deeply respected each other. But their first year of marriage was filled with what Janelle later referred to as "a thousand tiny surprises." None of these surprises were catastrophic; they were just unexpected — often amusing, sometimes confusing, occasionally frustrating.

Take weekend mornings.

Janelle grew up in a family where Saturdays meant slow breakfasts, long conversations, and peaceful lounging. Omar came from a home where Saturdays meant productivity: lawn mowing, errands, car maintenance, and ironing anything within reach. To him, sitting still felt like a waste of perfectly good sunlight.

For months they kept misunderstanding each other.

Janelle thought Omar's busyness meant he didn't want to relax with her.

Omar thought Janelle's stillness meant she didn't want to accomplish anything together.

Neither interpretation was true.

They simply had different internal settings.

One morning, after a small disagreement about how to spend the day, they finally named the root issue:

"I just assumed you would want what I want."

Assumptions — that was the real culprit.

They talked honestly about what rest and productivity each of them valued.

They compromised. They learned each other's rhythms.

Eventually, Saturdays became a blend: a little leisure, a little work, and a lot more understanding.

What began as tension became tenderness, not because their expectations disappeared, but because they were spoken, negotiated, and honored.

Where Expectations Come From

We don't invent expectations out of thin air. They come from a mixture of:

1. Family of origin

The homes we grew up in become our unconscious templates for what "normal" looks like.

2. Past relationships

Old patterns — positive or negative — tend to cast shadows on current dynamics.

3. Personality and temperament

Some people crave order; others thrive in flexibility. Some need routine; others need adventure.

4. Cultural influences

Movies, church teaching, social media, and even advertisements shape our ideas of romance and partnership.

5. Unseen fears and desires

Expectations often hide deeper needs — security, belonging, attention, affirmation, respect, stability.

Understanding the source of your expectations doesn't fix everything automatically. But it gives you context, and context softens conflict. When you know why something matters to your partner, it becomes easier to meet them with compassion instead of confusion.

Realistic Expectations vs. Unrealistic Ones

Not all expectations are created equal. Some are healthy and reasonable — mutual respect, honesty, kindness, emotional safety. These form the backbone of a healthy marriage.

Unrealistic expectations, however, often stem from pressure, fantasy, or fear:

- expecting your partner to anticipate needs you haven't expressed

- expecting them to consistently meet needs you haven't fully understood yourself

- expecting flawless emotional responses

- expecting romance to always feel effortless

- expecting conflict to be rare or painless

- expecting personal growth without discomfort

- expecting your partner to fill every emotional gap you carry

Unrealistic expectations turn good people into constant disappointments.

Realistic expectations make room for humanity — yours and theirs.

The Art of Shared Expectations

Healthy couples don't avoid expectations; they share them.

They talk about them.

They negotiate them.

They refine them.

They revisit them as life changes.

Shared expectations are a sign of *maturity*, not control. They protect the relationship from resentment and confusion.

A shared expectation might sound like:

"Let's both agree to communicate if we're running late."

"Can we talk through holidays and make a plan we both enjoy?"

"I need more verbal affection — can we work on that?"

"I'd love to find a better balance in chores."

"When we argue, can we both avoid getting sarcastic?"

These aren't demands.

They're invitations to mutual care.

When Expectations Clash

Not all expectations can coexist peacefully. Sometimes two good desires simply don't align. When that happens, couples move from "Who's right?" to "What do we need?"

This shift changes everything.

Differences don't have to be battles. They can be opportunities for creativity:

- maybe holidays rotate

- maybe chores get redistributed

- maybe weekends alternate between adventure and rest

- maybe affection styles blend

- maybe quiet needs and connection needs meet halfway

- maybe budgeting becomes a shared project instead of a solo burden

The goal isn't perfect agreement; it's shared understanding and shared effort.

The Spiritual Side of Expectations

Scripture invites us to humility, patience, and love — not perfection. It reminds us that we all "see through a glass dimly," meaning we all have blind spots. Expectations are part of that. We don't always know where our expectations come from or why they feel so strong.

- Grace gives us room to learn and grow.

- Love gives us courage to speak honestly.

- Humility keeps us open to being shaped by the person we love.

- And patience reminds us that marriage is a long journey, not a quick course.

When we treat expectations with gentleness instead of frustration, they become tools for connection rather than sources of conflict.

Reflection Questions

What expectations do you carry from your family or past relationships?

Which unspoken expectations have caused tension in your relationship?

What expectations do you hold that feel especially tender or important?

What expectations does your partner carry that you're just now understanding?

What is one expectation you could clarify together this week?

Homework for Chapter Fifteen

1. The Expectation Inventory

Each partner writes down three expectations they have about the relationship — one practical, one emotional, and one spiritual. Share and discuss them gently.

2. The "Why Does This Matter?" Conversation

Choose one expectation and explore the deeper need underneath it.

3. A Simple Prayer

"God, help us understand each other's needs with patience and grace."

Chapter Sixteen

Growing Together Instead of Growing Apart

Every marriage begins with two people who have chosen each other wholeheartedly. But life doesn't stay still. People change. Circumstances change. Jobs shift, bodies age, priorities evolve, families expand or contract, dreams adapt, and faith journeys deepen or take surprising turns. All of this is normal — even healthy. The real question isn't whether you and your partner will grow. It's whether you will find ways to grow together.

Growth isn't always dramatic. Sometimes it looks like emotional maturation, increased self-awareness, or greater empathy. Other times it looks like spiritual renewal, new hobbies, changing values, or new experiences. Growth can be slow and steady or sudden and disruptive. But whatever form it takes, it will shape your relationship.

Some couples fear change because they assume it means drifting apart. But change doesn't have to divide a relationship. In fact, shared growth is one of the most powerful bonds in marriage. When couples learn to honor each other's evolution and participate — even imperfectly — in each other's journeys, they create a partnership that is dynamic, resilient, and open to transformation.

Growing together is not about staying identical. It's about staying connected.

Why Couples Fear Growth

Many couples associate growth with instability. They worry, consciously or unconsciously, that if one partner evolves, the other will be left behind. Sometimes the fear is rooted in past experiences where change brought loss. Sometimes it comes from childhood patterns in which security depended on sameness. And sometimes it's simply fear of the unknown — a worry that if their partner becomes someone new, the relationship might not feel as familiar.

But resisting growth is like resisting the tide. It doesn't hold the shoreline together; it simply exhausts you.

Couples who thrive long-term learn to embrace change as an opportunity rather than a threat. They realize that growth doesn't destroy the foundation — it enriches it.

Meet Priya and Caleb

Priya and Caleb had been married nearly a decade when Priya began feeling drawn back into spiritual practices she hadn't engaged with in years. She started reading theology again, journaling, attending a small group, and exploring questions she never had time to wrestle with earlier in life. Meanwhile, Caleb was entering a season of professional changes that left him feeling unsure of his identity and purpose.

They loved each other, but suddenly it felt like they were each on a different journey. For a few months, their connection grew quieter. Not hostile — just muted. Priya worried her renewed spiritual curiosity made her sound overly intense. Caleb worried his vocational uncertainty made him sound lost. They didn't want to burden each other, so both tried to "figure things out privately."

Of course, privacy turned into distance.

One evening, while folding laundry, Priya finally spoke. She told Caleb she missed sharing life with him — not just day-to-day logistics but the deeper parts of who they were becoming. Caleb admitted he'd been afraid that opening up about his uncertainty would overwhelm her.

What came next wasn't dramatic: just a slow conversation about where they felt stretched and where they felt hopeful. That conversation didn't magically fix everything, but it reconnected them. It reminded them that growing together simply meant letting each other in.

Over the next year, they made space for each other's transformations. Priya invited Caleb into the more reflective parts of her spiritual life. Caleb invited Priya into his vocational questions. They didn't always understand each other's processes, but they understood the importance of witnessing them.

Their marriage deepened not because they solved everything, but because they chose to walk through change side by side.

The Three Types of Growth Every Couple Encounters

Growth usually shows up in three major areas:

1. Personal Growth

Emotional healing, increased self-awareness, therapy, spiritual curiosity, new hobbies, or developing healthier boundaries.

2. Relational Growth

Learning better communication skills, becoming more patient, improving conflict habits, or revisiting patterns that need repair.

3. Life-Stage Growth

Changes brought by career shifts, health issues, aging parents, empty nesting, parenting challenges, retirement, or major relocation.

Each type of growth requires attention. And each one creates opportunities for couples to either move closer or drift silently apart.

How to Grow Together Intentionally

Growing together doesn't require a detailed plan. It requires curiosity, communication, and presence. Here are some gentle ways couples can nurture shared growth:

1. Stay Interested in Each Other's Inner World

Ask about your partner's evolving thoughts, dreams, questions, or fears — not as an obligation, but as an act of love. People blossom when someone is genuinely curious about who they are becoming.

2. Make Room for Differences

Your partner's growth doesn't have to mirror your own. One might lean into spiritual exploration while the other leans into professional development. One might pursue creativity while the other focuses on mental health. The goal isn't sameness — it's companionship.

3. Revisit Your Shared Values

As you both change, some values deepen while others shift. Periodically revisit what matters to you: generosity, hospitality, adventure, faith, simplicity, community, justice, connection. Shared values become the compass in seasons of change.

4. Learn New Things Together

Take a class. Read a book at the same time. Try a new activity. Even small shared experiences help marriages stay emotionally agile.

5. Allow Each Other to Evolve

Grant your partner the freedom to change — even in ways that surprise you. A healthy marriage is spacious enough to hold two growing souls, not two stagnant versions of who you were years ago.

6. Talk About Change Before It Turns Into Tension

Instead of waiting until differences become resentments, create a habit of checking in about growth:

"What's changing inside you right now?"

"Where do you feel stretched or inspired?"

"What's something new you're discovering about yourself?"

This turns growth into connection rather than conflict.

What Happens When One Partner Grows Faster?

It's inevitable that periods of uneven growth will occur. One partner may be undergoing significant transformation while the other feels steady. Or one may feel stuck while the other is flourishing.

This unevenness is not a threat — it's an invitation to practice patience and empathy.

If your partner is the one evolving quickly, be curious rather than defensive. Ask what excites them or what feels uncertain. Celebrate their expansion.

If you're the one evolving, invite your partner into the journey gently, without expecting them to "catch up." Growth is not a race; it's a rhythm.

Remember: the goal is not synchronized timing. The goal is mutual support.

When Growth Brings Tension

Sometimes growth reveals unhealthy patterns that need attention — past wounds, conflict habits, or ways of communicating that no longer serve you. This can be uncomfortable, even painful. But it's also deeply fruitful.

Healthy couples don't fear tension that emerges from growth. They treat it as a signal that something important is rising to the surface. They talk. They listen. They adjust. They practice compassion.

Tension birthed from growth is not a sign of relational collapse. It's often a sign of relational renewal.

Spiritual Growth as a Shared Journey

Spiritual growth can be tender territory. People evolve differently in their relationship with God — sometimes in ways that challenge a couple's rhythm. One partner may feel drawn into prayer or Scripture while the other enters a season of doubt. One may crave more spiritual practices; the other may feel overwhelmed or uncertain.

This is where grace becomes essential. Honoring each other's spiritual path — wherever it is at the moment — builds trust. Instead of forcing shared spirituality, couples can create gentle opportunities to connect:

- praying together briefly

- attending a service occasionally

- sharing reflections from a book or sermon

- practicing gratitude daily

- engaging in acts of service together

Spiritual unity is not identical belief at identical moments. It is shared humility, shared honesty, and shared hope in God's presence through every season.

Reflection Questions

How have you changed in the past few years, and how has that shaped your relationship?

What changes has your partner experienced that you haven't fully understood yet?

Where do your growth paths intersect right now?

Are there areas where one of you feels left behind or unsupported?

What new practice or experience could help you grow together in the coming season?

Homework for Chapter Sixteen

1. The Growth Conversation

Take turns sharing one area where you feel yourself changing. Then share one area where you see growth in your partner.

2. Create a Shared Growth Goal

Choose a small goal to pursue together — reading a book, taking a class, attending a group, or simply discussing a topic regularly.

3. A Simple Prayer

"God, help us grow in ways that deepen our love and keep us rooted in grace."

Chapter Seventeen

Jealousy, Insecurity, and the Things We Don't Say Out Loud

Every relationship, no matter how strong, eventually brushes up against jealousy or insecurity. These emotions don't care how long you've been together, how committed you are, or how deep your love runs. They show up quietly at first — a tightening in the chest, a sudden shift in tone, a question you ask twice because the first answer didn't soothe you.

Jealousy and insecurity are not signs of weak love. They are signs of vulnerable love.

We only feel threatened when something matters to us.

We only feel insecure when we fear losing someone essential.

And we only feel jealous when part of us is unsure of our own worth.

These feelings are uncomfortable, but they're completely human. The danger isn't feeling them — it's burying them until they turn into resentment or distance.

Healthy couples learn to talk about jealousy and insecurity not with shame, but with honesty and tenderness. They learn to normalize the fact that even devoted partners sometimes feel afraid, and that naming those fears is an act of trust, not accusation.

Why Insecurity Shows Up Even in Healthy Marriages

Insecurity often has very little to do with what's happening in the present moment. It usually comes from something deeper — old wounds, past relationships, family messages, or moments in life when we felt invisible or replaceable.

Insecurity might emerge when:

- your partner seems distracted or distant

- they're excited about something that doesn't involve you

- someone else compliments them

- they succeed in an area where you feel self-critical

- you're going through a season of stress or self-doubt

- intimacy patterns shift

- friendships or outside commitments expand

- you notice changes in appearance, mood, or priorities

None of these triggers indicate actual danger. They simply expose a tender place inside you that still longs for reassurance.

The key is learning to share those tender places in a way that invites connection rather than reaction.

Meet Vanessa and Jordan

Vanessa and Jordan had a strong marriage — joyful, affectionate, rooted in deep friendship. But after Jordan started a new job, Vanessa found herself feeling uneasy around one of her coworkers. She wasn't proud of the feeling, and she certainly didn't want to seem controlling or insecure, so she kept it to herself at first.

The unease grew.

It wasn't logical — she trusted Jordan completely — but logic and emotion don't always share the same office space.

One evening she finally said, "I'm embarrassed to admit this, but I've been feeling... insecure lately." Jordan put down what she was doing and listened. Not defensively. Not dismissively. Just listened.

Vanessa explained that a harmless comment from his coworker had unexpectedly triggered old memories of a past relationship — the one where she'd felt easily replaced. It had nothing to do with Jordan. It had everything to do with the ache she still carried from years before.

Jordan didn't try to justify anything or explain it away.

She simply took her hand and said, "Thank you for telling me. I don't want you carrying that alone."

That conversation changed the emotional temperature immediately. Vanessa no longer felt ashamed of her feelings, and Jordan understood where her vulnerability came from. Jordan became a little more intentional about checking in during his busy weeks. Vanessa became more comfortable asking for reassurance.

It wasn't a dramatic breakthrough — it was a gentle one.

And gentle breakthroughs are often the ones that last.

The Healthy Side of Jealousy

There is a destructive form of jealousy — the kind that becomes controlling, accusatory, or isolating. But there is also a healthy form, one that simply signals:

"I love you deeply,

and I want to feel close to you."

Healthy jealousy is a longing for connection, not control. It's a reminder that your relationship is important, that you value intimacy, and that you want to feel secure. When expressed well, it creates closeness rather than conflict.

The difference lies in how you communicate it.

How to Talk About Jealousy or Insecurity Without Causing Damage

Talking about insecurity requires courage, humility, and a little preparation. Here's how couples can navigate it with grace:

1. Start with ownership

"I know this is my insecurity,"

rather than

"You're doing something wrong."

2. Focus on feelings, not accusations

"It made me feel uneasy,"

instead of

"You made me jealous."

3. Explain the deeper story

Sometimes the current situation is just the surface. Sharing the backstory helps your partner understand what's really happening emotionally.

4. Ask for reassurance gently

Most partners are glad to give reassurance; they simply don't know you need it unless you say so.

5. Stay open to their perspective

Your partner may not have realized something felt sensitive to you. That's okay. Give them space to respond without blame.

6. Keep the conversation calm

Strong emotions are understandable, but the calmer the conversation, the safer the outcome.

These conversations are not about assigning fault — they're about sharing vulnerability.

Being the Partner Who Hears the Insecurity

If your partner opens up about feeling insecure or jealous, the way you respond will either deepen trust or shut it down. Even if the insecurity seems irrational from your perspective, the feeling itself is real.

A loving response sounds like:

"Thank you for telling me."

"I can see this really matters to you."

"I don't want you to feel alone in this."

"How can I help you feel safer?"

It's not your job to fix every insecurity your partner carries. But it is your role to walk with them through it — gently, compassionately, consistently.

Sometimes your partner simply needs reassurance that you're here, that they matter, and that nothing is threatening the bond you share.

Reassurance is not enabling.

Reassurance is connection.

When Jealousy Turns Destructive

There are moments when jealousy crosses a line:

- demands to monitor each other

- accusations without evidence

- restricting friendships

- punitive behavior

- emotional manipulation

- attempts to control appearance, communication, or independence

These behaviors are not about love — they are about fear, and sometimes about power. If jealousy becomes controlling or demeaning, that's a sign deeper healing or professional support is needed.

Healthy jealousy seeks connection.

Unhealthy jealousy seeks control.

A loving marriage protects autonomy, trust, and dignity.

Healing Old Wounds Together

Many insecurities have roots long before the marriage began. Childhood experiences, past betrayals, losses, or family messages shape what we fear in adulthood. When couples talk openly about these histories, they begin to understand each other on a deeper level.

Healing becomes a partnership rather than a solo project.

You cannot undo your partner's past, but you can help reshape how it affects the present. You can become part of the safety they longed for long before you met.

When couples approach insecurity as shared work — not blame — old wounds lose power.

The Spiritual Side of Emotional Safety

Scripture again and again reveals God responding to human insecurity with reassurance:

"Do not fear, for I am with you."

"You are mine."

"I will never leave you or forsake you."

"I have loved you with an everlasting love."

In marriage, we echo a small reflection of that divine reassurance. We remind each other that we are valued, chosen, and cherished — even in the places where we feel the most fragile.

A marriage becomes spiritually grounded when partners feel safe enough to expose their fears, trusting they will be met with love rather than judgment.

Reflection Questions

What situations tend to trigger insecurity for you, and why?

How does jealousy show up in your relationship — quietly or visibly?

What kind of reassurance helps you feel grounded during vulnerable moments?

Are there parts of your partner's insecurity that you haven't fully understood yet?

What past experiences might still influence your reactions today?

Homework for Chapter Seventeen

1. Share One Vulnerability

Each partner names one insecurity they've been hesitant to talk about. Keep the tone gentle and curious.

2. Offer Intentional Reassurance

Give your partner one specific reassurance this week — something meaningful to their heart, not just yours.

3. A Simple Prayer

"God, help us meet each other's vulnerability with tenderness and understanding."

Chapter Eighteen

BALANCING "US" AND "ME"

One of the most delicate dynamics in any long-term relationship is learning how to be deeply connected without becoming absorbed, and how to remain fully yourself without becoming distant. It sounds simple, but it's one of the quiet arts of a healthy marriage — the art of balancing "us" and "me."

Every couple begins with two distinct people, each with their own histories, preferences, quirks, passions, and dreams. Over time, those two lives intertwine to form something new: the relationship itself — an "us" that becomes its own living thing. It has its own memories, rituals, language, rhythms, and history. That shared life is beautiful and powerful, but it isn't meant to replace the two individuals who created it.

Healthy marriages honor both:

the togetherness that builds intimacy,

and the individuality that keeps the relationship vibrant, curious, and alive.

Finding that balance takes intention — and occasionally renegotiation — because what each partner needs from "us" and from "me" changes across seasons of life.

Why This Balance Is Hard

Many of us carry unspoken messages from our upbringing about what partnership should look like. Some were taught that closeness means doing everything together. Others were taught that independence is the highest virtue. Still others grew up in homes where boundaries were unclear, leaving them unsure of how to balance connection and autonomy.

Add to that personality differences — one partner may crave closeness while the other needs personal space to feel grounded — and suddenly the landscape becomes much more nuanced.

The truth is, both closeness and independence are important. The challenge is learning to communicate what you need without making your partner feel rejected or smothered.

Meet Malcolm and Serena

Malcolm and Serena loved each other deeply but couldn't understand why they frequently ended up in the same argument. Serena loved shared activities: cooking together, evening walks, watching shows side by side, joint projects, and weekend outings. For her, togetherness was comfort.

Malcolm, on the other hand, needed periodic solitude to feel centered — time to read, work on hobbies, or just sit quietly with his thoughts. He loved being close to Serena, but after a full day around people, he needed personal time before he could re-engage.

Neither preference was wrong. They were simply different.

But because they hadn't talked about these needs openly, both interpreted the other's behavior through the wrong lens. Serena sometimes took Malcolm's need for solitude as disinterest. Malcolm sometimes felt overwhelmed by Serena's preference for connection and mistakenly assumed he was failing her.

Their breakthrough came during a long conversation in the backyard one evening. Malcolm explained that time alone actually helped him show up more fully for their marriage. Serena explained that shared time made her feel secure and connected. They realized that their needs weren't in conflict — they just needed better rhythm.

They decided to create a simple structure: three evenings a week dedicated to shared activities, two evenings reserved for individual time, and weekends approached with flexibility and communication. Once they understood each other's inner worlds, they stopped taking things personally and began supporting each other more intentionally.

Their marriage didn't change overnight — but their understanding of each other did. That made all the difference.

The Two Essential Questions

Healthy marriages often revolve around two steady questions:

1. What does our "us" need right now?

Maybe it needs more time, more presence, more affection, more laughter, or more intentional connection.

2. What do each of our "me's" need right now?

Maybe one partner needs solitude, creativity, friendships, movement, quiet, spiritual reflection, or rest.

Both questions matter equally.

And the answers shift over time.

There will be seasons when the relationship needs more attention — after a move, during grief, in early parenthood, or during a crisis. There will be seasons when individual pursuits need more room — career changes, personal growth, spiritual exploration, or deep rest.

The balance is dynamic, not static.

Independence Is Not Rejection

One of the most common misunderstandings in marriage is assuming that a partner's need for personal time is a withdrawal from connection. But healthy independence isn't rejection — it's renewal.

Your partner's individuality existed long before the marriage. It's part of what drew you to them in the first place: their interests, personality, talents, sense of self, and unique way of seeing the world. Those things shouldn't disappear once vows are exchanged. If anything, marriage should nurture them.

When partners make room for each other's individuality, they gain:

- more emotional resilience

- deeper appreciation

- richer conversations

- a sense of novelty and discovery

- lower resentment

- healthier attachment

You're not losing each other.

You're giving each other space to breathe — and breathe better together.

Togetherness Is Not Clinginess

Just as independence can be misunderstood, so can closeness. Wanting shared experiences isn't clinginess — it's connection. Wanting to spend time together isn't dependency — it's intimacy. Wanting to feel emotionally close isn't neediness — it's human.

Connection is the bond that allows a marriage to thrive. Without shared time, affection, and presence, even the most independent relationships grow lonely.

Healthy closeness looks like:

- shared rituals

- intentional quality time

- open conversation

- laughter

- touch

- vulnerability

- companionship

Closeness becomes unhealthy only when it replaces individuality — not when it complements it.

How Couples Find Their Balance

Finding the right blend of "us" and "me" isn't a one-time decision. It's a conversation that continues throughout your marriage.

Here are a few ways couples navigate this balance well:

1. Name What You Need Without Apology

Saying "I need some quiet time tonight" or "I'd love some time together this weekend" is an act of honesty, not selfishness.

2. Avoid Interpreting Needs as Threats

A request for time apart isn't a rejection.

A request for time together isn't a demand.

Treat needs as information, not criticism.

3. Create Rhythms, Not Rules

Patterns of connection and independence help your marriage feel predictable and safe without feeling rigid.

4. Encourage Each Other's Passions

When couples support each other's hobbies, callings, and friendships, they keep curiosity alive in the relationship.

5. Build Shared Dreams, Too

Even while pursuing personal passions, couples thrive when they have mutual goals — financial, spiritual, relational, or creative.

6. Revisit the Balance Regularly

Life changes. Needs change. What worked last year may not work now. Gentle recalibration keeps the relationship healthy.

When the Balance Feels Off

Sometimes couples drift into patterns that don't feel good — one person overwhelmed by constant togetherness, the other feeling abandoned by too much distance. When that happens, the solution is not blame but conversation.

Ask each other:

"Where do you feel connected right now?"

"Where do you feel disconnected?"

"Do you feel like you're getting enough personal space?"

"Do you feel like our relationship is getting enough attention?"

These questions open doors that silence quietly locks.

You don't need perfect alignment.

You just need awareness and willingness.

The Spiritual Wisdom of Interdependence

Scripture encourages community, connection, companionship, and mutual support — while also honoring solitude, retreat, and personal calling. Jesus himself practiced both. He withdrew to quiet places, then returned to people with renewed energy and compassion.

A healthy marriage mirrors this spiritual rhythm.

Two people, each created in the image of God, bringing their whole selves into a shared life while honoring the individuality God placed in each of them.

Marriage doesn't erase "me."

It weaves "me" and "me" into a sacred "us" that is stronger because of the individuality within it.

Reflection Questions

Do you tend to lean more toward connection or independence in your relationship?

What personal practices help you feel like yourself?

What shared practices help you feel close as a couple?

Where do you feel the balance is working well right now?

What part of the balance could benefit from a gentle adjustment?

Homework for Chapter Eighteen

1. The Balance Check-In

Each partner names one thing that helps them feel individually grounded and one thing that helps them feel relationally connected.

2. The Together/Separate Plan

Choose one activity to do together this week and one personal activity to make space for each other to enjoy separately.

3. A Simple Prayer

"God, help us hold each other with love and freedom, honoring both our individuality and our shared life."

Chapter Nineteen

MONEY, MEANING, AND THE STORIES WE CARRY

If love is the poetic side of marriage, money is the practical side — the part that can either create steady partnership or ignite conflict faster than you can say "interest rate." It's amazing how something made of paper and pixels can carry so much emotional weight. But it does, because money isn't just money. It's security, freedom, identity, hope, stress, opportunity, and sometimes, pure mystery.

Most financial conflict in relationships has very little to do with how much money a couple has. It has everything to do with what money means to each partner.

And those meanings are rarely the same.

Every person enters marriage with financial stories shaped by their upbringing, memories, wounds, fears, and dreams. Some people grew up in households where every dollar was accounted for and spending without a plan was unthinkable. Others grew up in families where money came and went unpredictably, so spending became a way to claim joy while it was available. Some absorbed messages about "being responsible." Others absorbed messages about "not being afraid to enjoy life."

All of these stories follow us into adulthood. And into marriage. And into arguments about whether we really needed the premium version of the streaming package.

Money is emotional. That's why it demands tenderness, not just spreadsheets.

Why Money Is Such a Sensitive Topic

Talking about money can stir up some of our deepest insecurities. It touches on:

- self-worth

- identity

- childhood wounds

- trust

- fear of scarcity

- fear of failure

- desire for control

- longing for security

- dreams of the future

It's no wonder people get tense when the topic comes up. Money is never just dollars — it's meaning. When couples argue about finances, they're often arguing about fear or longing, not math.

But there's good news:

Understanding each other's financial stories can turn money from a battleground into a place of partnership.

Meet Alicia and Thom

Alicia and Thom had been married for about a year when they discovered they had sharply different views on spending. Alicia loved planning — spreadsheets, envelopes, color-coded categories, the whole deal. Structure made her feel safe. Thom, on the other hand, felt anxious whenever life got too rigid. He'd grown up in a home where surprise expenses and sudden crises were the norm, so he learned to enjoy what he could when he could. To him, spending a little extra on something fun was a way to reclaim control over life.

Their arguments were rarely about the purchases themselves. They were about the emotions underneath.

One night, after a tense exchange over whether to save or spend their tax refund, they finally had the breakthrough conversation they'd been avoiding. Alicia confessed that her need for structure came from watching her parents nearly lose their home when she was a teenager. Thom admitted that his desire to enjoy the moment came from years of never knowing whether there would be anything to enjoy at all.

They finally realized:

They weren't fighting each other.

They were fighting their pasts.

That conversation didn't magically erase their differences. But it softened them. Understanding each other's stories made compromise possible. Soon they found a rhythm that honored both needs — stability and enjoyment, planning and play.

Their financial life became a partnership instead of a tug-of-war.

The Three Money Stories Every Couple Navigates

Every couple manages finances in the middle of three intersecting stories:

1. Your Story

The beliefs, fears, habits, and experiences you inherited about money.

2. Your Partner's Story

A completely different set of beliefs shaped by their world.

3. Your Shared Story

The new narrative you're writing together — the story that reflects who you are as partners rather than who you were as individuals.

This third story is where financial peace grows. It's where you craft shared values around generosity, saving, spending, giving, hospitality, security, and simplicity. It's where you learn to respect each other's instincts, even when they're different from your own.

Talking About Money Without Spiraling

Money conversations go badly fast when couples talk about behaviors instead of feelings. "Why did you spend that?" is a behavior question. "I feel anxious when our account dips below a certain amount" is a feelings question.

The difference is dramatic.

Healthy financial conversations sound like:

"This spending category feels stressful for me — can we talk about why?"

"What does saving represent to you?"

"What makes you feel financially secure?"

"What part of our money management feels overwhelming to you?"

"What are the goals we want to work toward together?"

Talking this way turns money into a shared responsibility instead of a source of blame.

Finding a Financial Rhythm That Works for Both of You

There's no universal formula that works for every marriage. But here are some principles that help couples find balance:

1. Honor Each Other's Emotional Needs

One partner may need structure; the other may need flexibility. When both needs are acknowledged, solutions become easier.

2. Create a Shared Plan

Budgets can be as simple or complex as you want. The point is agreement, not rigidity.

3. Revisit the Plan Regularly

Life changes. Jobs shift. Needs evolve. Money plans should be living documents.

4. Keep Transparency Non-Negotiable

Secrets around money erode trust faster than almost anything else.

5. Dream Together

Talk about travel, home projects, charity, retirement, adventure — anything that excites you both. Shared dreams make financial discipline feel purposeful.

6. Don't Forget Generosity

Giving — no matter how modest — strengthens a couple's sense of purpose and aligns the heart with gratitude rather than fear.

When Money Becomes a Source of Shame

Sometimes financial issues trigger shame — debt, mistakes, overspending, or years of poor habits. Shame makes people defensive or avoidant. But the remedy for shame is honesty and compassion.

If you are carrying shame around money, sharing it with your partner can transform isolation into connection. If your partner opens up about financial shame, receive their story with gentleness, not correction.

Shame loses its power when it's spoken aloud in a safe place.

The Spiritual Dimension of Finances

Jesus talked about money more than almost any other topic — not because he was obsessed with economics, but because he understood its emotional and spiritual power. Money reveals what we value, what we fear, and what we trust.

Healthy couples treat finances as a form of stewardship, not just an exchange of numbers. Stewardship includes generosity, responsibility, compassion, and gratitude. It also includes grace — grace for mistakes, grace for differences, and grace for the ongoing learning curve.

Financial unity becomes a spiritual practice, a way of saying together:

"We want to use what we have wisely, joyfully, and lovingly."

Reflection Questions

What money messages did you absorb growing up?

How do you typically feel when you discuss finances — anxious, relaxed, overwhelmed, hopeful?

What financial habits help you feel secure?

What dreams do you want to prioritize together?

What emotional need sits underneath your financial style?

Homework for Chapter Nineteen

1. The Money Story Conversation

Share one childhood memory related to money that still shapes how you feel today.

2. Create One Shared Financial Goal

Choose something small and achievable — like saving for a weekend trip or paying off a small debt together.

3. A Simple Prayer

"God, guide our hands, our resources, and our hearts as we build a life rooted in wisdom, generosity, and peace."

Chapter Twenty

HOW TO REALLY TALK (AND ACTUALLY FEEL HEARD)

Most couples think they're pretty good communicators — at least until the first misunderstanding hits harder than expected. Then communication suddenly becomes one of those mysterious skills everyone assumes they're born with, like knowing how to fold a fitted sheet or remembering where you parked at Costco.

Communication is one of the most misunderstood parts of marriage. People often think communication means getting your point across. But healthy communication is much more about connection than content. It's not just the exchange of words — it's the sharing of meaning, emotion, nuance, intention, and trust.

Good communication says, "I want to understand you."

Great communication says, "I want you to feel understood."

Those are two very different things.

The goal isn't to win arguments or to be right. The goal is to build a bridge between two hearts that don't always think, feel, or process life the same way.

And when communication works, something beautiful happens:

Even hard conversations become places of closeness instead of conflict.

Why Communication Breaks Down

Most communication issues aren't actually about the words spoken — they're about what's happening under the words. Tone, timing, emotional energy, assumptions, and past experiences all mingle together in a way that can either bring clarity or create confusion.

Common breakdowns include:

- speaking from stress instead of intention

- assuming your partner "should already know"

- trying to resolve conflict when one person is overwhelmed

- using defensive or protective humor

- interrupting instead of listening

- shutting down when emotions rise

- talking around an issue instead of naming it

- expecting mind-reading instead of clarity

None of these behaviors mean a marriage is failing. They mean two humans are being human.

Meet Clara and Devonte

Clara and Devonte had a marriage full of love, humor, and shared values — yet they kept running into communication problems that left them both feeling misunderstood. Clara processed emotions by talking things through immediately; Devonte processed by retreating into silence until he gathered his thoughts.

Both approaches were valid, but they kept colliding.

One evening after a long day, a minor misunderstanding escalated faster than either of them expected. Clara felt that Devonte was shutting her out. Devonte felt Clara was demanding answers he wasn't ready to give. They weren't angry at each other — they were overwhelmed by the difference in how they communicated.

Eventually, after each taking a breather, they sat down and talked about the pattern. Clara explained that silence made her feel abandoned. Devonte explained that immediate discussion made him feel trapped. For the first time, they understood that the issue wasn't personal — it was neurological. Their emotional processing styles simply ran at different speeds.

Together they developed a simple strategy:

When tension arose, Devonte would say, "I need twenty minutes to clear my head. I'm not leaving the conversation — I'm getting ready for it."

Clara would reply, "Okay. I'll be ready when you are."

That one adjustment changed everything. Suddenly the space Devonte needed wasn't interpreted as distance, and the connection Clara needed wasn't interpreted as pressure. Their communication found a rhythm — one built on respect instead of reaction.

Listening Is More Than Hearing

If communication is a bridge, listening is the foundation. But listening well is harder than people admit. It requires patience, presence, and a willingness to pause your internal reactions long enough to understand your partner's perspective.

Healthy listening looks like:

- making space for the whole story

- asking clarifying questions

- reflecting back what you heard

- resisting the urge to fix immediately

- letting go of defensiveness

- listening for emotion, not just information

When couples practice this kind of listening, conversations feel safer, deeper, and more productive.

Listening says:

"I'm here.

I'm with you.

And your experience matters to me."

Speaking with Kindness and Clarity

How we speak to each other shapes the emotional climate of the relationship. Tone matters as much as content. Timing matters as much as tone. And intention matters most of all.

Some gentle principles:

1. Start soft, not sharp

A soft start creates openness. A sharp start triggers defensiveness.

2. Say what you mean, not what you fear

Fear says: "You never listen to me."

Truth says: "I'm feeling unheard. Can you help me understand what's going on?"

3. Use "I" statements

"I feel..."

"I need..."

"I'm confused..."

This creates connection instead of blame.

4. Avoid absolute language

"You always..." and "You never..." are almost always untrue and always unhelpful.

5. Focus on one issue at a time

Dragging five old arguments into a new one never leads to resolution.

6. Give the benefit of the doubt

Assume your partner's intentions are good unless proven otherwise.

Kindness doesn't weaken communication.

It strengthens it.

Understanding Each Other's Communication Styles

People communicate based on temperament, culture, upbringing, past relationships, and emotional wiring. Learning these differences makes communication smoother, kinder, and less personal.

For example:

- Some people need time to process.

- Others think out loud and need interaction.

- Some communicate logically.

- Others communicate emotionally.

- Some prefer calm discussion.

- Others express passion through intensity.

- Some need structure.

- Others need freedom to express themselves organically.

No style is "better."

The key is adaptation — learning to speak in a way your partner can actually receive.

Good communication isn't rigid.

It's flexible and generous.

Timing Matters More Than Most People Realize

A conversation that goes terribly at 10 p.m. might go beautifully at 10 a.m. The same topic brought up during a moment of exhaustion, hunger, stress, or distraction can fail simply because the window wasn't right.

Healthy couples learn to ask:

"Is this a good time to talk?"

And they learn to respect the answer.

This one skill protects countless marriages from unnecessary conflict.

Repairing Communication After a Misstep

Every couple has moments when communication dissolves — voices rise, feelings get hurt, timing collapses, intentions get misunderstood. The couples who thrive are not the ones who communicate perfectly, but the ones who repair quickly and kindly.

Repair sounds like:

"I'm sorry — I didn't communicate that well."

"Can we try that again?"

"I didn't mean to shut down."

"I shouldn't have raised my voice."

"I love you. Let's reset."

Repair isn't about blame.

It's about restoring connection.

The Spiritual Side of Communication

Scripture is full of cautions about the tongue and reminders about the power of words — to bless, to build, to heal. Communication becomes sacred when couples use it not as a weapon, but as a way to honor God and each other.

Words can be bridges or barriers.

They can open hearts or close them.

They can create unity or sow division.

Healthy communication is one of the clearest ways a couple reflects Christlike love — patient, kind, slow to anger, rich in understanding, deep in compassion.

Reflection Questions

How did your family communicate when you were growing up?

What communication habits do you bring into the relationship that work well?

Which habits sometimes get in the way?

What helps you feel safe during a hard conversation?

What helps you feel heard?

Homework for Chapter Twenty

1. The "Tell Me More" Practice

Choose a topic — any topic — and spend five minutes practicing active listening. The listener's only job is to say, "Tell me more."

2. The Kindness Reset

This week, if a conversation starts off tense, pause and restart it gently.

3. A Simple Prayer

"God, guide our words so they build connection, trust, and understanding."

Chapter Twenty-One

FRIENDSHIP: THE SECRET STRENGTH OF EVERY GREAT MARRIAGE

Long before romance settles into its comfortable rhythm, long after the early excitement transforms into deeper love, and long before the hard seasons have fully run their course, something quieter holds a marriage together: friendship.

Marriage is often talked about in terms of passion, commitment, or shared values. Those matter deeply. But friendship — steady, warm, affectionate friendship — is the part that makes a relationship feel like home. It's the foundation that steadies the storms, the cushion that softens the difficult days, and the spark that keeps the relationship playful and alive.

When couples talk about why they fell in love, the stories vary. But when couples talk about why they stayed in love, the reasons almost always come down to friendship — the way they laugh together, enjoy each other's company, share inside jokes, trust each other with their vulnerabilities, and experience life as partners rather than opponents.

Friendship doesn't replace romance or deep emotional intimacy. It supports them. Without friendship, marriage becomes a contract. With friendship, it becomes companionship — the kind God intended when God said, "It is not good for the human to be alone."

Why Friendship Matters So Much

Romantic love can surge and recede, sometimes dramatically. Seasons of stress, grief, parenthood, career challenges, or personal change can dim the intensity of romantic expression. Passion is important, but it's rarely consistent. Friendship, however, is steady. Friendship is the thread that remains strong even when everything else feels uncertain.

Friendship brings:

- gentleness

- humor

- patience

- empathy

- shared history

- mutual encouragement

- deep trust

These are the qualities that make a marriage resilient — not just beautiful, but durable.

And unlike passion, which sometimes requires the right conditions, friendship can thrive almost anywhere. It grows through small interactions, daily rituals, tiny moments of connection.

Meet Ivy and Mateo

Ivy and Mateo met at a community volunteer event, long before either of them considered the idea of dating. They bonded first over humor — a shared ability to make each other laugh in places where silence was preferred — and then over long conversations. Their early friendship carried a warmth that felt effortless.

When they eventually began dating and married, that friendship became the anchor of their relationship. Years later, during a season that tested them emotionally — a difficult job loss, a move, and a serious illness in the family — they relied more heavily on their friendship than ever before.

Some days they were too tired for romance or deep conversation. But they were never too tired to be friends.

Mateo once said, "We don't always have fireworks, but we always have coffee in the morning and a walk in the evening. That's our glue." Ivy added, "And humor. Honestly, humor has saved us in more ways than counseling."

They weren't minimizing the challenges they faced. They were simply naming a truth: friendship kept their connection alive through seasons when other parts of the relationship were stretched thin.

Their story isn't unusual. Many couples find that friendship is the part of their marriage that carries them through the hardest chapters — not because it's dramatic, but because it's faithful.

What Friendship in Marriage Actually Looks Like

Friendship isn't abstract or complicated. It shows up in dozens of ordinary ways:

- enjoying each other's company without needing entertainment

- laughing at the same things

- checking in on each other throughout the day

- knowing each other's quirks and loving them

- creating inside jokes that live for years

- teasing lightly without wounding

- encouraging each other's dreams

- offering comfort without being asked

- being honest, even when it's difficult

- supporting each other's weird hobbies

- showing up when you're needed — even quietly

- trusting each other with fears and hopes

Friendship looks a lot like kindness.

A lot like consistency.

A lot like presence.

It's not glamorous, but it's profoundly meaningful.

When Friendship Starts to Fade

Friendship doesn't disappear overnight. It fades through neglect — through busyness, stress, resentment, exhaustion, or drifting emotional habits. Couples don't mean for it to fade. It just slips into the background while life demands attention elsewhere.

Signs friendship might need renewal include:

- going long periods without laughing together

- losing interest in each other's daily experiences

- more screen time than shared time

- conversations becoming purely functional

- feeling more like co-managers than companions

- avoiding vulnerable topics

- losing the sense of fun

The good news?

Friendship is one of the easiest parts of a marriage to revive. It doesn't require dramatic gestures. It requires renewed attention and presence.

Rekindling Friendship (Even If It's Been a While)

Here are gentle, realistic ways to rebuild friendship:

1. Start talking about small things again

Not every conversation needs to be deep. Sharing interesting stories, observations, or the funny thing that happened at work brings back lightness.

2. Laugh intentionally

Humor is healing. Watch something funny together. Share memes. Revisit old inside jokes. Laughter reconnects people without demanding vulnerability.

3. Spend casual time together

This can be as simple as a walk, coffee, a game, or sitting outside. Unstructured time helps couples rediscover ease.

4. Show curiosity

Ask questions you haven't asked in years. Interests evolve. So do dreams. Get reacquainted.

5. Play

Playfulness makes friendship feel alive — board games, spontaneous outings, cooking experiments, anything that breaks routine.

6. Revisit shared memories

Tell stories from your past. Look at old pictures. Reminisce about your early days. It strengthens your sense of "us."

Friendship is won through small gestures repeated often — not grand efforts done occasionally.

Friendship Doesn't Replace Romance — It Deepens It

Couples sometimes worry that strong friendship means their relationship feels "more friendly than romantic." But the truth is that romance often grows best in the soil of friendship.

When couples feel emotionally safe, seen, appreciated, and supported — romance has room to breathe. Friendship doesn't diminish desire; it strengthens it. It keeps the relationship from becoming transactional or resentful.

Romance eventually fluctuates.

Friendship holds steady and invites romance to return gently.

The Spiritual Depth of Friendship

Scripture has a high view of friendship — the kind of loyalty and commitment that mirrors the heart of God. Jesus called his disciples friends, not servants. Ruth clung to Naomi in a devotion that shaped the lineage of Christ. Proverbs describes friends who stick closer than siblings.

Marriage blends all kinds of love — companionship, spiritual partnership, affection, passion — but friendship is often the most Christlike part. It's patient, kind, humble, forgiving, and loyal. It shows up even when passion is tired and communication is strained.

Friendship is the everyday holiness of marriage.

Reflection Questions

Which aspects of friendship come naturally to you as a couple?

What parts of your friendship have drifted in recent years?

What do you genuinely enjoy doing together — even in small doses?

How do you show each other warmth, humor, or companionship?

What is one way you could strengthen your friendship this week?

Homework for Chapter Twenty-One

1. Plan a Friendship Date

Not a romantic date — a friendship date. Something fun, low-pressure, and enjoyable for both of you.

2. Share a Memory

Tell each other one story from early in your relationship that still makes you smile.

3. A Simple Prayer

"God, strengthen our friendship so it carries joy into every part of our marriage."

Chapter Twenty-Two

PATIENCE: THE SLOW WORK OF LOVE

If love is the heartbeat of a marriage, patience is the breath — quiet, steady, sustaining, often unnoticed until its absence becomes glaring. Most of us don't enter a relationship thinking, "I can't wait to become a more patient person." Yet marriage has a way of revealing exactly where patience is needed, and sometimes where it's in short supply.

Patience isn't a passive virtue. It's not simply "gritting your teeth until the storm passes." It's an active posture of the heart — a willingness to give your partner room to grow, space to learn, freedom to be imperfect, and time to become the person they are becoming. Patience is humility and compassion in motion.

It's also surprisingly practical. Patience keeps conflict small instead of explosive, misunderstandings repairable instead of lingering, and habits flexible instead of rigid. Marriage requires countless micro-moments of patience — the kind you won't get credit for, the kind no one else sees, the kind that shows up in small graces repeated day after day.

Why Patience Is Hard (Even for Loving People)

Patience is difficult because we're human. We all have blind spots, emotional triggers, fears, assumptions, and habits we've been carrying since childhood. We're wired for comfort, routine, and predictability — and marriage, ironically, requires constant adjustment.

We struggle with patience not because our partners are unbearable, but because our expectations for how quickly change should happen don't always align with reality. We want progress faster. We want clarity immediately. We want our partner to understand something right away, even if it took us years to recognize in ourselves.

And then there's the other factor: the pace of life. When we're tired, stressed, hungry, overwhelmed, anxious, or stretched thin, our patience shrinks. Sometimes dramatically. Marriage confronts us with this truth regularly — not to shame us, but to invite a gentler, more spacious way of relating.

Meet Rory and Kim

Rory and Kim adored each other, but patience was not their shared strength. Rory tended to process emotions quickly — sometimes too quickly, resulting in rushed apologies or premature conclusions. Kim processed slowly and carefully, needing time to reflect before responding.

This difference turned small conversations into points of frustration. Rory felt anxious when Kim took too long to answer. Kim felt pressured when Rory wanted immediate clarity. Both loved each other deeply, but their differences in emotional timing repeatedly left them feeling misunderstood.

The turning point came when Kim explained that when she asked for time, it wasn't avoidance — it was protection. She wanted to offer a thoughtful, truthful response, not something spoken in haste. Rory admitted that his urgency came from fear — fear of losing connection, fear of conflict lingering, fear that silence meant rejection.

Simply naming these fears softened them. They began to understand that patience wasn't about waiting forever — it was about trusting the process. Rory learned to give Kim space without assuming the worst. Kim learned to reassure Rory that space didn't mean distance. Over time, their conflict became gentler, their conversations deeper, and their relationship more peaceful.

Their story is hardly unique. Many couples discover that patience isn't the ability to wait — it's the ability to wait with love.

Patience Creates Emotional Safety

A patient heart communicates something powerful:

"You are allowed to be human around me."

When your partner senses patience — real, grounded patience — they feel free to express confusion, sadness, frustration, anxiety, or doubt without fear of judgment. They feel safe enough to show their imperfect parts, knowing they won't be punished or shamed.

Impatience, on the other hand, tends to shut people down. It makes vulnerability risky. It creates pressure, defensiveness, or silence. Emotional safety shrinks quickly when partners feel rushed, dismissed, or criticized for their pace of growth.

Healthy marriages cultivate patience because healthy marriages cultivate safety.

Patience During Hard Seasons

Every long-term relationship encounters difficult seasons — health challenges, job loss, grief, depression, parenting stress, spiritual uncertainty, family tension, or major life transitions. These seasons stretch patience to its limits.

But patience during hard times is the glue that keeps a marriage from unraveling. It reminds both partners that they don't have to "bounce back" quickly or pretend they're fine when they're struggling. Patience gives time for healing. It gives permission to be fragile. It allows grief, confusion, and limitation to be part of the story.

Sometimes patience looks like sitting silently beside someone who is hurting.

Sometimes it looks like accepting that your partner won't have energy for much beyond survival.

Sometimes it looks like giving reassurance repeatedly, even when you've said it before.

Sometimes it looks like not taking things personally when your partner is overwhelmed.

Patience during these seasons becomes a form of love that is deeper than romance — a love rooted in endurance and compassion.

Patience for Growth and Change

Marriage isn't static. People evolve. And not always at the same speed. You may go through a season of emotional growth or spiritual awakening while your partner feels stuck or uncertain. Or vice versa.

This uneven pace can create tension if patience is missing. But with patience, unevenness becomes an opportunity to support rather than resent. Patience says:

"I'm here for you at the pace you're capable of."

This doesn't mean tolerating harmful behavior or unhealthy patterns indefinitely. It means giving each other breathing room to grow without demanding instant transformation.

Growth almost never happens on a timeline. Patience acknowledges that — and embraces the journey.

Communicating Needs with Patience

Patience doesn't mean staying silent about your needs. It means communicating them without urgency, accusation, or pressure. It means speaking truth with gentleness.

Patience says:

"I need something from you,

but I love you enough to express it kindly

and trust you enough to let it take time."

Often the most powerful conversations in marriage happen when patience and honesty work together — when you express your needs clearly but hold space for your partner to respond at their own pace.

Patience gives honesty a soft landing.

The Spiritual Side of Patience

Scripture repeatedly calls patience a fruit of the Spirit — something that grows within us as God shapes our heart. Patience is holy not because it is quiet or polite, but because it reflects the nature of God's love: slow to anger, abounding in compassion, willing to walk with us through every phase of transformation.

Marriage becomes sacred when partners treat each other with that kind of patience. Not perfection. Not constant serenity. But a willingness to slow the pace of judgment and speed up the pace of compassion.

Patience is love stretched across time.

Reflection Questions

What situations in your relationship tend to challenge your patience the most?

What does patience look like to you — emotionally, spiritually, and practically?

How do you respond when your partner needs more time to process something?

Where could a little extra patience strengthen your connection right now?

What kind of patience do you most appreciate receiving?

Homework for Chapter Twenty-Two

1. The Patience Conversation

Each partner shares one area where they're working on growth and invites the other to be patient during that process.

2. The Patience Practice

Choose one daily interaction where you will intentionally slow down and respond with extra gentleness.

3. A Simple Prayer

"God, teach us the patient love that frees us to grow, to heal, and to care for each other with grace."

Chapter Twenty-Three

HEALTHY BOUNDARIES: LOVING EACH OTHER WITHOUT LOSING YOURSELF

When most people hear the word "boundaries," they imagine something cold or restrictive — walls, distance, or emotional withdrawal. But in healthy relationships, boundaries are not barriers. They're bridges. They're the structures that allow two people to love each other without losing themselves, and to stay close without collapsing into one tangled emotional knot.

Boundaries protect the relationship by protecting the individuals within it.

They say, "This is who I am. This is what I need. This is where I'm learning. This is how I stay emotionally healthy."

Every long-term couple — queer, straight, or anywhere on the beautiful spectrum of human love — has to navigate boundaries. Not because love is fragile, but because intimacy requires clarity. You cannot love someone fully if you don't understand where their tender edges are, what overwhelms them, or where they need breathing room.

Boundaries aren't about separation.

They're about sustainability.

Why Boundaries Matter in Marriage

Marriage (or any committed partnership) brings emotional closeness unlike any other relationship. You share dreams, routines, meals, responsibilities, bed space, fears, hopes, bodies, and families. Your lives intertwine in beautiful and complicated ways.

But that closeness can become overwhelming without structure. A relationship can crumble under:

- unspoken expectations

- emotional fusion

- resentment

- caretaking instead of supporting

- unhealthy dependence

- unclear roles

- guilt-driven generosity

- lack of personal space

- fear of disappointing one another

Healthy boundaries prevent these dynamics by defining what is helpful, what is harmful, and what keeps each partner grounded.

Boundaries don't diminish intimacy.

They deepen it.

Meet Lillian and Harper

Lillian and Harper had a deeply loving marriage, full of affection, humor, and commitment. But they kept running into a particular problem: Harper tended to absorb other people's emotions, especially Lillian's. If Lillian was stressed, Harper was stressed. If Lillian was worried, Harper was worried. If Lillian had a bad day, Harper felt responsible for fixing it.

Harper's intentions were loving, but the emotional merging left both partners exhausted. Lillian felt guilty — like she had to hide her stress to protect Harper. Harper felt overwhelmed — carrying burdens that weren't theirs to carry.

Finally, after one particularly intense week, they talked openly about the pattern. Lillian said, "I love how much you care, but I don't need you to rescue me. I just need you to sit with me, not carry me."

Harper admitted that growing up, they were the emotional caretaker in their family, which made them assume it was their job in the marriage too.

Together, they set new boundaries:

Lillian would express her emotions without expecting Harper to fix them.

Harper would offer support without absorbing the emotional weight.

The shift was gentle, but it changed everything. They still loved each other fiercely — but with more breathing room.

What Boundaries Actually Do

Healthy boundaries create:

1. Emotional Clarity

You know what your partner is feeling and what you are feeling.

2. Healthier Conflict

Instead of reacting from overwhelm, you can respond from groundedness.

3. Better Support

You give compassion without overextending yourself.

4. More Authenticity

You don't have to pretend, hide emotions, or mask your needs.

5. More Respect

You understand each other's limits and honor them.

6. Less Resentment

Nobody is silently sacrificing or carrying more than they can handle.

Boundaries reduce confusion and increase compassion.

Common Boundary Challenges in Couples

Every couple navigates different dynamics, but here are some of the most common:

1. Time Boundaries

Balancing togetherness and personal time.

2. Emotional Boundaries

Supporting your partner without absorbing their emotions as your own.

3. Family Boundaries

Navigating parents, siblings, in-laws, chosen family, or extended family expectations.

4. Social Boundaries

Balancing friendships, hobbies, and community with time together.

5. Physical Boundaries

Respecting comfort levels with touch, intimacy, space, energy, and rest.

6. Digital Boundaries

Phones, screens, texting habits, social media use, privacy expectations.

7. Spiritual Boundaries

Honoring differences in belief, practice, or religious background.

8. Work Boundaries

Knowing when work ends and relationship time begins.

Each of these areas requires clarity — because unclear boundaries create unintentional hurt.

Healthy Boundaries Are Loving, Not Harsh

Unhealthy boundaries sound like:

"I'm done. Figure it out yourself."

"That's your problem, not mine."

"I don't want anything to do with that."

Healthy boundaries sound like:

"I care deeply about you. Here's what I'm capable of right now."

"I want to support you, but I need a moment to gather myself first."

"I love you, and here's the kind of help I can give tonight."

"I'm here with you, even if I can't fix this."

Healthy boundaries preserve dignity, connection, and safety.

How Couples Can Create Strong, Loving Boundaries

1. Talk About Limits Before You Hit Them

Don't wait until you're overwhelmed, resentful, or burned out. Boundaries are clearest when spoken early.

2. Use Clear, Gentle Language

"I need a twenty-minute break."

"I'm getting overwhelmed — can we pause?"

"I want to talk about this, but I need a clearer head."

"I can listen for a while, but then I need to rest."

Soft tone, clear message.

3. Notice Unrealistic Expectations

If you find yourself thinking "I shouldn't need rest" or "I should always be available," check that belief. It might be leftover wiring from earlier in life.

4. Practice Mutual Respect

When one partner names a limit, the other honors it — not grudgingly, but lovingly.

5. Revisit Boundaries Often

Life changes. Emotional needs change. Capacity changes. Couples grow stronger when they adjust boundaries rather than assuming yesterday's limits still apply.

6. Remember That Saying No Creates Space for a Better Yes

Saying no to overwhelm means you can say yes to healthy connection.

Boundaries and Identity

Healthy boundaries protect individuality. They say, "I am me, and you are you, and our differences enrich our relationship rather than threaten it."

Whether a couple is gay, straight, queer, or any beautiful constellation of identities, every relationship thrives when each partner feels safe to:

- have opinions

- have passions

- have friendships

- have emotional and spiritual needs

- have space to breathe

- have autonomy

Boundaries honor personhood — which strengthens partnership.

The Spiritual Wisdom of Boundaries

Even Jesus practiced boundaries.

He rested.

He withdrew from crowds.

He said no.

He protected his mission.

He didn't let others define his identity.

He honored his limits.

He sought quiet, solitude, and clarity.

If the Son of God needed boundaries, we definitely do.

Boundaries are a sacred expression of truthfulness — the honest acknowledgment of who we are and what we can give in any season. They make love sustainable, not strained.

Reflection Questions

Which types of boundaries come naturally to you as a couple?

Which ones feel difficult to maintain?

Do you ever feel overwhelmed, overextended, or responsible for things that aren't yours to carry?

How comfortable are you expressing a limit to your partner?

How do you respond when your partner expresses a limit to you?

Homework for Chapter Twenty-Three

1. The Boundary Inventory

Each partner lists three limits they have — emotional, physical, or time-related. Share them gently.

2. Practice a Healthy Boundary

Choose one small boundary to communicate this week ("I need a quick breather," "Let's revisit this later," etc.).

3. A Simple Prayer

"God, give us the wisdom to honor each other's limits and the courage to speak our own with love."

Chapter Twenty-Four

REPAIRING AFTER CONFLICT: THE ART OF COMING BACK TOGETHER

Every couple — truly every couple — fights. Some fights are quiet and tense, others are loud and emotional, and some are so petty you can only laugh about them two hours later ("Did we really just argue about who loads the dishwasher correctly?").

Conflict isn't a sign that something's wrong with your marriage.

It's a sign that two imperfect humans are learning how to love each other in real time.

But here's the truth:

It's not the conflict that determines the health of a marriage.

It's the repair that follows.

Repair is the emotional and relational glue that makes conflict safe instead of destructive. It's the soft landing after a hard moment — the gentle reminder that you're on the same team, even when you disagree. Couples who repair well don't avoid tension; they simply refuse to let it linger and harden into distance.

Repairing after conflict is not a neat, scripted process. It's an art. And like all arts, it improves with practice, patience, and a bit of humility along the way.

Why Repair Is Essential

Unrepaired conflict doesn't go away. It sinks into the emotional floorboards of a relationship, collecting in the gaps until the entire structure feels uneven. Even small disagreements, when left unresolved, can accumulate into resentment, insecurity, or emotional distance.

Repair does three vital things:

1. It restores connection.

Conflict disrupts emotional closeness. Repair rebuilds it.

2. It creates safety.

When partners know reconciliation is possible, arguments feel less frightening.

3. It deepens trust.

Repair teaches you that even hard moments don't break the bond.

Couples who master repair don't avoid conflict — they recover from it.

Meet Shawn and Elena

Shawn and Elena loved each other deeply, but their conflict style had a predictable pattern: Shawn expressed emotion quickly and intensely, while Elena needed space to process. She would withdraw to breathe; he would pursue for clarity. This dance often escalated their disagreements rather than resolving them.

After one particularly difficult argument — the kind rooted in both exhaustion and misunderstanding — they found themselves sitting on opposite ends of the couch, frustrated but silent. Hours later, they finally talked about something neither had fully acknowledged:

They didn't actually know how to repair.

"I want to come back together," Shawn said, "but I don't know when it's the right time, or what I'm supposed to say without making it worse."

"I want to reconnect too," Elena answered, "but when things get heated, I'm afraid anything I say will be the wrong thing."

Their breakthrough didn't come from analyzing the argument — it came from learning the mechanics of reconciliation. They created a simple ritual:

Elena would signal when she was ready to talk.

Shawn would approach with a softer tone.

They'd each start with, "Here's what I wish I had said instead..."

And they'd end with some small gesture of closeness — a hand-hold, a hug, or sitting together quietly.

It wasn't magical, but it worked.

Their fights didn't disappear. Their recovery improved.

That's the heart of healthy repair: not perfection, but restoration.

Repair Begins With Softening

Most couples need a moment to soften before they can repair — a shift in emotional temperature that makes connection possible again. Softening doesn't mean admitting fault before you're ready; it means showing willingness:

- lowering your tone

- relaxing your shoulders

- shifting body language

- speaking gently

- taking a breath before responding

Softening signals:

"I'm not your adversary. I'm your partner."

This alone opens the door for healing.

The Five Ingredients of Healthy Repair

1. Ownership

Not of the entire conflict — just of your part. Even if your contribution was small, naming it builds trust.

"I shouldn't have raised my voice."

"I got defensive, and I'm sorry for that."

Ownership is never weakness. It's emotional leadership.

2. Empathy

Understanding how your partner felt, even if you didn't intend to create that feeling.

"I can see why that was hurtful."

"I understand you felt overwhelmed."

Empathy softens hurt.

3. Curiosity

Gentle, open-ended questions that invite deeper understanding:

"Help me understand what you were feeling earlier."

"What did I miss in that moment?"

Curiosity turns a fight into a learning moment.

4. Reassurance

Conflict can trigger fears. Reassurance calms them.

"We're okay."

"I'm not going anywhere."

"We're on the same team."

Reassurance makes connection feel safe again.

5. A Gesture of Repair

A touch, a hug, a kind word, an offered hand, sitting together, an apology note later — anything that restores closeness.

Repair isn't complete until connection is renewed.

What Repair Is Not

It's important to note what repair isn't, because many couples accidentally sabotage reconciliation without realizing it.

Repair is not:

- rehashing the argument from scratch

- proving who was right

- minimizing the other person's feelings

- offering a "sorry" that shifts blame ("I'm sorry you mis-understood")

- rushing the process before emotions are ready

- pretending nothing happened

- using humor to avoid accountability

Repair is gentle, humble, and honest.

When Conflict Is Still Too Hot to Repair

Sometimes the emotions are simply too fresh. In that case, both partners need space — but healthy space, not punitive withdrawal.

Healthy space sounds like:

"Let's take a break and come back in thirty minutes."

or

"I need a moment to calm down, but I'm not abandoning the conversation."

This kind of space comforts rather than threatens.

Unhealthy space sounds like:

"I'm done."

"I don't care anymore."

or

walking away without saying anything.

One creates safety.

The other creates fear.

Couples often need to practice this distinction.

Apologies That Heal Instead of Hurt

A meaningful apology has three parts:

1. "I'm sorry for..."

Be specific. Identify the behavior, not the personhood.

2. "I understand that it made you feel..."

This validates your partner's internal experience.

3. "Next time I will..."

Repair without repair-plan leads to repeat conflict.

A good apology is not self-shaming. It's self-awareness.

The Spiritual Side of Repair

Scripture places astonishing value on reconciliation — not perfection, not avoiding conflict, but restoring peace. Jesus taught that reconciliation matters so much that one should "leave the gift at the altar" to pursue it. Paul wrote that we should "make every effort to keep the unity of the Spirit in the bond of peace."

Marriage is one of the most sacred places where reconciliation plays out. When partners come back to each other after conflict, they participate in the work of grace — not because they're perfect, but because they choose connection over pride.

Repair is holy work.

Reflection Questions

How do you typically approach repair after conflict?

What makes it difficult for you to soften after a disagreement?

What helps you feel safe enough to reconnect after a tense moment?

What form of apology feels most meaningful to you?

What repair gesture from your partner makes you feel loved?

Homework for Chapter Twenty-Four

1. Practice a Soft Start

After a minor disagreement, pause, breathe, and begin the repair process with gentleness.

2. Share Your Repair Language

Each partner says what kind of repair gesture helps them feel reconnected — a hug, a calm conversation, reassurance, humor, etc.

3. A Simple Prayer

"God, guide our hearts toward reconciliation, and help us repair with grace, humility, and love."

Chapter Twenty-Five

FORGIVENESS: HEALING WITHOUT PRETENDING

If there's one topic that gets romanticized, oversimplified, and occasionally weaponized in relationships, it's forgiveness. People often imagine forgiveness as a simple moment — a soft sigh, a gentle nod, maybe a hug, and everything is magically fine again. In reality, forgiveness is one of the most demanding forms of love. It asks us to acknowledge pain, confront disappointment, and let go of bitterness, all while staying open to connection.

Forgiveness is not pretending the hurt didn't happen.

It's not sweeping issues under the rug.

It's not forcing a smile while resentment grows underground.

And it's not giving your partner a free pass to repeat the same patterns endlessly.

Forgiveness is a healing journey — honest, imperfect, sacred — that frees both partners to move forward with integrity.

Why Forgiveness Takes Time

Humans aren't wired to immediately release pain. Emotional wounds take time to settle and integrate. When we're hurt by our partner — the one person who sees the deepest parts of us — the pain can feel sharper because intimacy amplifies everything: the joy, the vulnerability, and yes, the hurt.

Forgiveness takes time because:

- trust needs rebuilding

- the nervous system needs calming

- the heart needs reassurance

- old wounds sometimes get triggered

- fear of recurrence needs addressing

- meaning needs clarity ("Why did this happen?")

Forgiveness is not just an emotional release; it's a rebuilding project.

And rebuilding is slow.

Meet Andre and Melissa

Andre and Melissa were in a solid, loving marriage when an unintentional but painful breach of trust shook them harder than either expected. Andre had forgotten to follow through on something promised — something Melissa needed for an emotionally significant reason. It wasn't malicious, but it mattered deeply.

Melissa felt unseen, dismissed, and unimportant. Andre felt horrible, defensive, and ashamed. Their communication spiraled, and for several days they lived in emotional limbo — still connected, but tender in all the wrong places.

What finally changed everything was a long, honest conversation on a quiet Sunday afternoon. Melissa said, "I want to forgive you, but I need some space to trust that this won't happen again." Andre responded, "I understand. And I want to earn that trust back, not rush you into giving it."

That moment — the naming of the wound, the humility, the consent for time — created a healing pathway. Over the next few weeks, Andre made deliberate efforts to show reliability. Melissa softened gradually, not because she forced herself to, but because she genuinely felt seen and valued again.

Their journey wasn't linear. There were days when old fear resurfaced. But each time, they came back to the same truth: forgiveness takes commitment, not hurry.

What Forgiveness Is

Forgiveness is a complex, tender process that includes:

1. Acknowledging the Hurt

You cannot forgive what you refuse to admit. Naming the pain honestly is essential.

2. Understanding the Impact

It's not about intention — it's about effect. Understanding how your partner felt builds empathy.

3. Choosing Release

Forgiveness doesn't erase memory; it releases resentment's hold on the heart.

4. Creating Repair

Change, effort, responsibility — these make forgiveness sustainable.

5. Rebuilding Trust Slowly

Trust returns in steps, not leaps.

Forgiveness is *not* forgetting.

It's healing.

What Forgiveness Is Not

Forgiveness is not:

- pretending everything is fine

- allowing harmful patterns to continue

- suppressing feelings

- excusing behavior without accountability

- forced reconciliation

- bypassing emotional reality

Forgiveness without truth is fragile.

Forgiveness without repair is temporary.

The Role of Apology in Forgiveness

A meaningful apology is one of the most powerful tools in the forgiveness process. It opens the door for healing and signals genuine responsibility. An apology is not just words; it's a posture.

A true apology includes:

1. Naming the behavior

"I'm sorry I snapped at you."

"I'm sorry I broke that promise."

2. Naming the impact

"I see how it hurt you."

"I understand why it shook your trust."

3. Commitment to change

"Here's how I'll make sure it doesn't happen again."

4. Openness to accountability

"You can tell me if I'm slipping. I want to grow."

Performance apologies — the ones meant to quiet conflict rather than repair it — can do more harm than good. Real apologies heal because they honor the truth.

Forgiving Yourself, Too

Couples often focus on forgiving each other, but sometimes the harder work is forgiving ourselves. When we've made mistakes, hurt someone we love, or fallen short of our own expectations, shame can linger long after the conflict has passed. Shame whispers that we are unworthy of love, incapable of change, or destined to repeat our failures.

But shame is not truth. Shame isolates. It hides. It erodes intimacy by telling us we're not safe enough to be honest.

Self-forgiveness makes room for growth. When we offer ourselves the same grace we offer our partner, we create a relationship where humanity is welcome — not punished.

Forgiveness and Boundaries

Forgiveness does not mean resetting everything back to zero. It means healing while still honoring what needs protecting going forward. Sometimes that means clearer agreements, new rhythms, or healthier boundaries.

Forgiveness is the softening of the heart.

Boundaries are the strengthening of the relationship.

Both are necessary.

Rebuilding Trust After a Deep Hurt

Trust is a fragile thing: slow to build, quick to shatter, slow to rebuild. Whether the hurt is small or significant, trust needs intentional care to return.

Rebuilding trust involves:

- transparency

- consistency

- follow-through

- reliability

- reassurance

- accountability

- openness to feedback

Trust is not restored by promises.

Trust is restored by patterns.

And patterns take time.

Spiritual Dimensions of Forgiveness

Forgiveness is central in Christian spirituality, not because God asks us to minimize pain, but because God understands that unforgiveness chains the heart. Scripture depicts forgiveness as a pathway to freedom — not just for the person being forgiven, but for the one doing the forgiving.

Forgiveness in marriage is a sacred practice. It echoes God's patient compassion, God's willingness to keep showing up, God's tender insistence that grace is stronger than failure.

But remember this:

Even Jesus didn't romanticize forgiveness. He acknowledged wounds, confronted injustice, and restored gently. His model of forgiveness was truthful and healing — not rushed or naive.

That is the kind of forgiveness marriages thrive on.

Reflection Questions

What makes forgiveness difficult for you at times?

How do you usually respond when you're hurt — do you withdraw, get defensive, or seek clarity?

What kind of apology helps you feel understood?

What fears come up when you think about offering forgiveness?

What steps help you rebuild trust when it's been shaken?

Homework for Chapter Twenty-Five

1. The Forgiveness Conversation

Talk about one past hurt — large or small — that still needs softening. Approach it gently and without blame.

2. Practice a Repair Ritual

Choose a small gesture (a hug, a prayer, a phrase, a handhold) that you use intentionally after moments of tension.

3. A Simple Prayer

"God, heal the places where hurt lingers, and help us offer forgiveness with honesty, courage, and compassion."

Chapter Twenty-Six

INTIMACY ACROSS SEASONS: STAYING CLOSE WHEN LIFE CHANGES

Most couples enter a relationship with a fairly simple understanding of intimacy. Early on, closeness feels natural, frequent, and almost effortless. Desire is high, curiosity is strong, and time together often feels abundant. Intimacy flows easily because life hasn't yet demanded much negotiation.

Then life happens.

Careers change. Bodies change. Stress levels fluctuate. Health issues arise. Parenting enters the picture — or doesn't, but caregiving still does. Faith evolves. Energy shifts. Schedules tighten. And intimacy, once spontaneous, begins to require intention.

None of this means something has gone wrong.

It means your relationship is alive and moving through seasons.

Intimacy is not a static experience. It's a living conversation between two people who are constantly changing. Healthy couples don't expect intimacy to look the same forever — they learn how to tend it through each chapter of life.

Redefining Intimacy Beyond the Beginning

One of the most damaging myths couples absorb is the idea that "real intimacy" should always feel the way it did at the beginning. When that doesn't happen, couples often internalize unnecessary shame or anxiety.

But early intimacy is fueled by novelty and discovery. Long-term intimacy is fueled by safety, trust, and emotional depth. These are different energies — both beautiful, but not interchangeable.

Intimacy over time becomes richer, not weaker, when couples allow it to mature. It deepens as partners learn each other's rhythms, vulnerabilities, bodies, boundaries, and emotional landscapes. But that depth requires curiosity, communication, and patience.

Long-term intimacy isn't automatic.

It's cultivated.

Meet Theo and Marcus

Theo and Marcus had been together for over a decade when they realized something had shifted in their intimate life. They still loved each other deeply. They laughed easily. They supported each other through work stress and family challenges. But physical intimacy had become less frequent and more tentative.

Neither knew how to bring it up.

Theo worried that mentioning it would sound like criticism. Marcus worried it would confirm his fear that something was "wrong" with him. So they avoided the conversation — not out of disinterest, but out of care.

Eventually, during a quiet evening at home, Marcus finally said, "I miss feeling close to you — not just physically, but emotionally too." Theo admitted he felt the same, and that stress and exhaustion had quietly taken center stage in his life.

That conversation didn't magically restore everything overnight. But it opened the door. They began talking honestly about energy, desire, expectations, and fears — without blame. They learned that intimacy didn't have to look like it used to in order to be meaningful.

Over time, they rebuilt closeness in new ways: intentional time together, gentle touch without pressure, shared rituals of affection, and honest conversations about desire. Their intimacy became slower, more tender, and deeply connected.

What they lost in spontaneity, they gained in trust.

Intimacy Is More Than Physical

Physical intimacy matters. It is one of the unique gifts of romantic partnership. But intimacy itself is broader and more layered than sex alone.

Intimacy includes:

- emotional openness

- shared vulnerability

- physical affection

- meaningful conversation

- mutual presence

- playful connection

- spiritual closeness

- feeling seen and desired

- feeling safe and accepted

When couples struggle with physical intimacy, the root is often emotional disconnection, exhaustion, unresolved tension, or fear — not lack of attraction. Addressing intimacy holistically creates space for healing without pressure.

When Desire Doesn't Match

One of the most common challenges couples face is mismatched desire. One partner may want more physical connection, while the other feels overwhelmed, tired, anxious, or disconnected. This mismatch can quietly breed resentment if it isn't handled with care.

Desire is influenced by:

- stress

- mental health

- physical health

- trauma history

- hormones

- body image

- emotional safety

- unresolved conflict

- exhaustion

- self-worth

Desire is *not* a measure of love.

It's a response to the conditions surrounding us.

Healthy couples talk about desire without shaming each other. They approach the conversation with curiosity instead of pressure. They ask, "What helps you feel close?" rather than "Why don't you want this?"

When desire feels mismatched, the goal is not winning or convincing. The goal is understanding.

Creating Safety Around Intimacy

Intimacy thrives in safety. When partners feel pressured, judged, or inadequate, desire shuts down. When partners feel respected, affirmed, and emotionally secure, intimacy has room to grow.

Creating safety looks like:

- honoring boundaries

- respecting "no" without punishment

- separating intimacy from obligation

- communicating needs gently

- avoiding comparison

- offering reassurance

- staying emotionally present

Safety invites openness.

Pressure invites withdrawal.

Couples who prioritize safety build intimacy that lasts.

Intimacy During Stressful Seasons

There are seasons when intimacy naturally takes a back seat — grief, illness, caregiving, financial stress, parenting exhaustion, depression, or major life transitions. These seasons require tenderness rather than panic.

Intimacy doesn't disappear during hard times. It transforms.

Sometimes intimacy looks like:

- holding hands in silence

- sitting together after a long day

- offering comfort without expectation

- sharing fears honestly

- choosing rest over performance

These forms of closeness are not lesser. They are deeply intimate in their own way.

Relearning Each Other Over Time

Bodies change. Energy changes. Needs change. Long-term intimacy requires relearning each other — again and again.

That means asking questions you may not have asked in years:

"What helps you feel close lately?"

"What makes intimacy feel stressful right now?"

"What kind of affection feels good to you these days?"

"What do you need more of — or less of?"

Curiosity keeps intimacy alive.

Assumptions slowly suffocate it.

Spiritual Intimacy and Shared Meaning

For many couples, intimacy is strengthened through shared spiritual practices — prayer, reflection, service, gratitude, or meaningful conversation about values and purpose. Even couples who differ in belief can nurture spiritual intimacy by honoring each other's inner life.

Spiritual intimacy reminds couples that their connection is not just physical or emotional, but deeply human and sacred.

It says:

"I see your soul, not just your body."

That kind of recognition deepens every other form of closeness.

When Intimacy Needs Extra Support

Sometimes intimacy struggles signal deeper wounds — trauma, chronic stress, depression, anxiety, shame, or unresolved conflict. Seeking support is not failure. It's wisdom.

Couples counseling, sex therapy, spiritual direction, or medical consultation can help couples navigate intimacy with compassion and clarity. Getting help says, "This relationship matters enough to tend carefully."

Reflection Questions

How has intimacy in your relationship changed over time?

What helps you feel emotionally and physically close right now?

Are there unspoken expectations around intimacy that need gentler conversation?

How do stress and exhaustion affect your sense of closeness?

What kind of intimacy feels most nourishing in this season of life?

Homework for Chapter Twenty-Six

1. The Intimacy Check-In

Set aside time to talk about closeness — without agenda, pressure, or problem-solving. Simply listen.

2. Practice Gentle Affection

Choose one form of non-demanding affection this week — a handhold, a hug, shared quiet time.

3. A Simple Prayer

"God, help us nurture intimacy with patience, tenderness, and grace, honoring each other fully in every season."

Chapter Twenty-Seven

Shared Purpose: Building a Life That's Bigger Than Both of You

At some point in every long-term relationship, a quiet question begins to surface. It doesn't always arrive in words, and it doesn't always announce itself dramatically. Often it shows up as restlessness, fatigue, or a vague sense that something meaningful is missing.

The question is this:

What are we building together?

Couples can love each other deeply and still feel unmoored if their shared life lacks direction. Romance, companionship, and intimacy matter — but most relationships need something more to feel grounded over time. They need shared purpose. Not a rigid mission statement, but a sense that the relationship is oriented toward something meaningful beyond day-to-day survival.

Shared purpose doesn't mean couples must agree on everything or pursue identical callings. It means they recognize that their partnership itself has a direction — a way of being in the world that reflects their values, hopes, and commitments.

Purpose gives love a horizon.

Why Shared Purpose Matters

When couples lack shared purpose, life can begin to feel transactional. Conversations revolve around schedules, responsibilities, logistics, and stress. The relationship becomes efficient, but not necessarily meaningful. Partners may feel like they're maintaining a system rather than nurturing a living bond.

Shared purpose does something different. It reminds couples why they chose each other in the first place. It provides a sense of "we" that transcends chores, calendars, and conflict.

Purpose brings:

- motivation during hard seasons

- resilience during disappointment

- perspective during conflict

- meaning during monotony

- hope during uncertainty

It answers the question, "Why does this relationship matter — not just to us, but in the larger story of the world?"

Meet Rowan and Elise

Rowan and Elise had a loving, stable marriage, but after several years together they began to feel oddly disconnected. Nothing was wrong. They communicated well. They supported each other. They handled conflict reasonably. But something felt flat.

One evening, after another long discussion about work stress and household logistics, Rowan finally said, "I feel like we're really good at surviving life together — but I don't know what we're aiming at."

That comment landed gently, but honestly.

Over the next few weeks, they began talking about what mattered most to them — justice, hospitality, creativity, faith, rest, generosity, and community. They realized they shared a deep longing to live generously and stay connected to people on the margins of their community.

They didn't overhaul their lives overnight. Instead, they started small. They opened their home more often. They volunteered together occasionally. They made intentional choices about where their time and energy went.

Slowly, their relationship felt alive again — not because they fixed something broken, but because they remembered what they were building together.

Purpose didn't replace love.

It gave love direction.

Shared Purpose Looks Different for Every Couple

There is no universal template for shared purpose. What matters is not what your purpose is, but that it is intentional and shared.

Shared purpose might include:

- raising children with certain values

- creating a home marked by hospitality

- serving a faith community

- pursuing justice or advocacy

- building a creative life together

- caring for extended family

- supporting one partner's calling

- living simply and generously

- cultivating deep friendships

- tending land, animals, or community spaces

- being a safe place for others

Some couples express purpose outwardly. Others express it quietly. Some focus on service. Others focus on creativity or stability or care. None of these are better than the others.

Purpose doesn't need to be impressive.

It needs to be authentic.

When Purpose Is Uneven

Often, one partner feels a stronger pull toward purpose than the other — at least initially. One may articulate vision more easily. One may feel restless while the other feels content. This imbalance doesn't mean the relationship is misaligned. It simply means the conversation needs space.

Purpose develops through dialogue, not pressure.

If you're the one feeling restless, speak from longing rather than frustration. If you're the one feeling content, listen without assuming your partner is dissatisfied with you. Purpose conversations aren't about blame; they're about alignment.

Couples grow closer when they explore purpose together rather than demanding agreement.

Purpose Evolves Over Time

What felt purposeful early in a relationship may change. Seasons shift. Energy changes. Values deepen. Life circumstances alter priorities. Purpose is not fixed — it's responsive.

Healthy couples revisit questions like:

"What matters most to us right now?"

"Where do we feel called to invest our energy?"

"What feels life-giving in this season?"

"What feels draining?"

"What do we want our relationship to stand for?"

These conversations keep the relationship aligned with reality rather than nostalgia.

Purpose and Faith

For couples shaped by Christian faith, shared purpose often emerges from spiritual values — love of neighbor, justice, compassion, hospitality, service, humility, and grace. But even when couples differ in belief or practice, shared purpose can still be deeply spiritual.

Purpose grows whenever couples orient their relationship toward something life-giving, compassionate, and meaningful. It grows whenever they ask not only, "What do we want?" but also, "How do we want to live?"

Shared purpose reflects the belief that love is not just for comfort, but for contribution.

Small Acts, Big Meaning

Shared purpose doesn't require dramatic gestures. Often it's expressed through small, faithful acts repeated over time:

- showing up for people consistently

- choosing integrity over convenience

- practicing generosity within limits

- creating spaces of welcome

- offering kindness when it's inconvenient

- staying rooted when leaving would be easier

These acts shape a relationship that feels grounded and intentional.

Purpose doesn't shout.

It endures.

When Purpose Feels Lost

There are seasons when purpose feels distant — during grief, burnout, illness, or transition. During these times, the purpose may simply be survival, care, and rest. That is not failure. That is faithfulness.

Sometimes the most sacred purpose is staying present, tending each other gently, and trusting that direction will return when strength does.

Purpose waits patiently.

Reflection Questions

What gives your relationship a sense of meaning right now?

Where do you feel restless or longing for something more?

What values do you share most deeply as a couple?

How do you want your relationship to impact others, if at all?

What small step could help you live more intentionally together?

Homework for Chapter Twenty-Seven

1. The Purpose Conversation

Set aside time to talk about what you feel called toward — without trying to solve or decide everything.

2. Choose One Shared Action

Pick one small practice that reflects your shared values — volunteering, hospitality, generosity, creativity, or rest.

3. A Simple Prayer

"God, guide our shared life toward what is meaningful, compassionate, and true."

Chapter Twenty-Eight

WEATHERING THE STORMS: STAYING CONNECTED WHEN LIFE GETS HARD

Every couple, no matter how loving or committed, will face seasons they never anticipated. Some storms arrive suddenly — a diagnosis, a loss, a job change, a betrayal of expectations. Others gather slowly — chronic stress, emotional fatigue, caregiving demands, financial pressure, spiritual uncertainty. No relationship is immune to hardship, because no life is free from it.

What distinguishes couples who endure is not the absence of storms, but the way they move through them together.

Hard seasons test a relationship's emotional infrastructure. They reveal how partners communicate under pressure, how they handle fear and uncertainty, how they offer support when they themselves are depleted, and how they make meaning out of suffering without turning against each other. Storms don't invent problems; they reveal what's already there — and they also reveal strengths couples didn't know they had.

This chapter is not about heroic endurance or "powering through." It's about staying connected — emotionally, relationally, spiritually — when life feels heavy and the future feels uncertain.

Why Hard Seasons Feel So Disorienting

Difficult seasons disrupt more than routines. They disrupt assumptions — about safety, fairness, control, and predictability. Couples often find themselves grieving not only what they've lost, but what they expected life to be.

Hard seasons can bring:

- fear and anxiety

- exhaustion and burnout

- irritability and short tempers

- emotional withdrawal

- grief and sadness

- loss of identity or purpose

- strain on intimacy

- differences in coping styles

None of these mean a relationship is failing. They mean human nervous systems are under stress.

When couples understand this, they are less likely to personalize each other's reactions. They stop interpreting stress responses as character flaws or relational rejection and begin seeing them for what they are: signals that care and gentleness are needed.

Meet Nadia and Chris

Nadia and Chris had built a solid, affectionate partnership. They communicated well, enjoyed each other's company, and shared a strong sense of purpose. Then Chris developed a chronic health condition that altered their daily life almost overnight.

Suddenly, routines changed. Energy levels dropped. Plans became uncertain. Medical appointments replaced date nights. Both partners felt scared — but in different ways. Chris felt grief over the loss of independence and identity. Nadia felt fear and responsibility, unsure how to support without losing herself.

They didn't argue much, but they grew quieter. Conversations became practical rather than emotional. Each partner tried to protect the other by withholding their fears.

Eventually, during a late-night conversation neither planned, Nadia admitted she felt lonely even while being physically present every day. Chris confessed feeling like a burden, terrified that needing help would erode their partnership.

That honesty changed everything.

They began naming the storm instead of tiptoeing around it. They learned that staying connected didn't mean always being strong — it meant being truthful. They found new rhythms: gentler intimacy, shared humor, intentional rest, and permission to grieve together.

Their relationship didn't return to what it was before.

It became something deeper — slower, more tender, and more honest.

Different Coping Styles, Same Storm

One of the biggest challenges during hardship is that partners often cope differently. One may want to talk constantly; the other may withdraw. One may seek reassurance; the other may need space. One may want to plan; the other may feel paralyzed. One may turn to faith; the other may wrestle with doubt.

These differences can feel threatening if couples assume there is a "right" way to suffer.

But coping differences are not betrayals. They are adaptations.

Healthy couples learn to say:

"This is how I cope."

"This is how you cope."

"Let's make room for both."

Understanding coping styles prevents unnecessary conflict and helps couples support rather than judge each other.

Staying Emotionally Connected Under Pressure

When life gets hard, emotional connection requires intentional effort. Stress narrows focus. Exhaustion reduces capacity. Fear makes people protective. That's why couples must be deliberate about staying emotionally tethered.

Connection doesn't require long conversations or dramatic gestures. Often it looks like:

- checking in regularly

- asking, "How are you really doing today?"

- sharing fears honestly

- offering reassurance without trying to fix everything

- acknowledging loss

- validating each other's emotions

- staying physically present, even in silence

Connection during hardship is less about solutions and more about solidarity.

Avoiding the Trap of Emotional Isolation

Many couples unintentionally isolate during hard seasons. They stop sharing feelings to avoid burdening each other. They retreat into self-protection. They focus on logistics and survival. Over time, emotional distance grows — not because love has faded, but because vulnerability feels too risky.

Isolation often sounds like:

"I don't want to make this harder for you."

"You already have so much on your plate."

"I should handle this on my own."

While well-intentioned, these thoughts quietly erode intimacy.

Suffering shared becomes suffering softened.

Suffering hidden becomes suffering multiplied.

Grief Has Many Faces

Grief isn't limited to death. Couples grieve lost expectations, lost health, lost opportunities, lost dreams, lost certainty. And grief does not move in a straight line.

Partners may grieve differently — one expressing sadness openly, the other processing internally. One may move toward acceptance sooner, while the other cycles through anger or despair. These differences can create misunderstanding if not named with compassion.

Grief requires patience — with yourself and with each other.

There is no timeline for grief.

There is only presence.

Intimacy During Hard Seasons

Hard seasons often affect intimacy — emotionally and physically. Stress and grief can dampen desire, shift energy, or create fear around closeness. Couples sometimes worry that this means intimacy is "broken."

It isn't.

It's adapting.

Intimacy during hardship may look different:

- gentle touch instead of sexual expression

- closeness without expectation

- emotional vulnerability replacing physical intensity

- reassurance replacing performance

- These forms of intimacy are not lesser. They are deeply connecting in their own way.

- Letting Others Help

Couples often believe they should be able to handle everything together. But isolation makes hardship heavier. Allowing trusted friends, family, faith communities, counselors, or support groups to help is not a failure — it's wisdom.

Support expands capacity.

It preserves energy.

It protects the relationship.

Letting others help allows couples to remain partners rather than becoming overwhelmed caretakers.

Faith, Doubt, and Meaning

Hard seasons often shake spiritual foundations. Some partners lean more deeply into faith; others feel disoriented or angry. Both responses are human. Healthy couples make room for spiritual difference without panic.

Faith during hardship isn't about tidy answers. It's about presence — trusting that God meets people in confusion, grief, and unanswered questions.

For couples, spiritual connection during hardship might look like:

- shared prayer or silence

- lighting a candle

- reading a psalm

- sitting together in stillness

- naming gratitude amid pain

- allowing doubt to coexist with faith

God is not threatened by honest struggle.

When Hard Seasons Change the Relationship

Some storms permanently alter a relationship's shape — caregiving roles, financial dynamics, energy levels, or life direction. These changes require grief, adjustment, and re-negotiation.

Healthy couples acknowledge loss rather than pretending nothing has changed. They mourn together. They adjust expectations. They redefine what partnership looks like now.

Love that adapts is love that lasts.

Hope Is Not Denial

Hope doesn't mean pretending things will magically improve. It means trusting that connection, meaning, and love are still possible — even in altered circumstances.

Hope sounds like:

"We don't know what comes next, but we're not alone."

"This is hard, and we're still here together."

"We will keep choosing each other."

Hope isn't loud.

It's faithful.

Reflection Questions

How do you and your partner typically respond to stress or crisis?

What hard season have you already navigated together, and what did you learn?

Where do you feel emotionally connected right now? Where do you feel distant?

What support outside your relationship might help during difficult times?

What helps you feel hopeful, even when answers are unclear?

Homework for Chapter Twenty-Eight

1. Name the Storm

Talk openly about a current or past hard season and how it affected each of you.

2. Practice Presence

Choose one daily practice that reinforces togetherness — a check-in, a walk, a shared moment of quiet.

3. A Simple Prayer

"God, hold us steady when life feels uncertain, and help us remain tender toward one another through every storm."

Chapter Twenty-Nine

CHOOSING EACH OTHER AGAIN AND AGAIN

Most couples remember the moment they first chose each other. It might have been a first date that lingered longer than expected, a conversation that felt surprisingly safe, or a quiet certainty that this person mattered in a way others hadn't. Early love often feels like a decision made once — enthusiastic, hopeful, and full of promise.

But long-term love isn't sustained by a single choice.

It's sustained by many small choices, made repeatedly, often quietly, and sometimes when choosing each other is the hardest thing in the room.

Marriage — or any committed partnership — is not a one-time vow. It's a practice. A daily orientation of the heart. A willingness to say, again and again, "I choose you, even here."

This chapter is about that choosing — not as romantic idealism, but as lived faithfulness.

Why Choice Matters More Than Chemistry

Chemistry is powerful. It ignites connection, fuels attraction, and makes early love feel effortless. But chemistry alone cannot carry a relationship through decades of change. Chemistry responds to feeling; choice responds to commitment.

Choice shows up when:

- feelings are complicated

- circumstances are exhausting

- communication is strained

- attraction ebbs

- disappointment lingers

- stress dominates

- certainty feels distant

Choice doesn't replace emotion — it anchors it. It creates a container in which love can mature rather than evaporate when conditions change.

Choosing your partner does not mean suppressing feelings. It means honoring the relationship even when feelings fluctuate.

Meet Sam and Jordan

Sam and Jordan had weathered many seasons together — career shifts, family tension, and the slow, sometimes unglamorous work of building a shared life. But during a particularly draining year, they noticed something unsettling: they had stopped choosing each other intentionally.

They still functioned well. Bills were paid. Responsibilities were handled. But connection had thinned. Conversations were efficient rather than curious. Affection was present but automatic. Both felt lonely — not dramatically, just quietly.

One evening, after yet another discussion about schedules and logistics, Jordan said, "I miss us choosing each other — not just running the household."

That sentence lingered.

Over the following weeks, they began to notice how often they defaulted to autopilot. They realized that while they hadn't chosen against each other, they also hadn't been actively choosing for each other. Love hadn't disappeared — intention had.

So they made small changes. They paused before reacting. They reintroduced simple rituals. They asked better questions. They offered affection deliberately. None of it was dramatic. But it was meaningful.

Choosing each other didn't feel grand.

It felt grounding.

The Myth of Effortless Love

Many couples quietly carry the belief that if love is "right," it shouldn't require effort. When effort becomes visible, they worry something has gone wrong. But effort doesn't signal failure. It signals investment.

Every meaningful thing requires attention — careers, friendships, spiritual life, health. Love is no different. The effort required changes over time, but it never disappears entirely.

Effort in love looks like:

- listening when you're tired

- repairing after conflict

- showing patience during growth

- practicing forgiveness

- staying curious

- offering reassurance

- making time

- choosing kindness when irritation would be easier

These are not signs of a struggling relationship.

They are signs of a living one.

Choosing Each Other in Small Moments

Grand gestures are memorable, but relationships are shaped in ordinary moments. The choice to stay present in a difficult conversation. The choice to soften instead of harden. The choice to ask rather than assume. The choice to reach for your partner instead of withdrawing.

Small choices accumulate.

Choosing each other might look like:

- putting the phone down

- asking how the day really went

- offering a hug before advice

- checking tone before speaking

- remembering what matters to your partner

- apologizing first

- choosing generosity over scorekeeping

These choices don't make headlines.

They make marriages.

When Choosing Feels Hard

There are seasons when choosing your partner feels natural and joyful — and seasons when it feels heavy. Stress, unresolved hurt, exhaustion, grief, or disappointment can make the choice feel costly.

In these seasons, choice is not about pretending everything is fine. It's about honesty paired with commitment. It's about saying, "This is hard, and I'm still here."

Choosing does not mean tolerating harm or erasing boundaries. It means staying engaged in the work of the relationship rather than abandoning it emotionally.

Sometimes choosing looks like seeking help.

Sometimes it looks like slowing down.

Sometimes it looks like renegotiating expectations.

Sometimes it looks like rest.

Choosing is flexible.

It adapts to reality.

Choosing During Conflict

Conflict is one of the clearest places choice becomes visible. Every disagreement presents a crossroads: protect yourself or protect the connection. Win the argument or tend the relationship. React or respond.

Choosing your partner during conflict doesn't mean avoiding disagreement. It means staying relational even while addressing tension.

It sounds like:

"I care about you, even though we disagree."

"Help me understand your perspective."

"Let's take a break and come back to this."

"I don't want to hurt us while we're hurting."

Conflict handled with choice becomes a place of growth rather than fracture.

Choosing After Hurt

Choosing each other after hurt is one of the bravest acts in a relationship. Hurt tempts withdrawal. It whispers that protection requires distance. Choosing, instead, says, "Healing matters more than retreat."

This does not mean rushing forgiveness or ignoring pain. It means staying open to repair. It means allowing the relationship to be a place of healing rather than permanent damage.

Choosing after hurt often unfolds slowly — through conversations, accountability, reassurance, and time. It is not a single moment. It is a series of decisions to keep the door open.

Choosing When Growth Is Uneven

Couples rarely grow at the same pace. One partner may be changing rapidly while the other feels steady. One may be questioning deeply while the other feels grounded. These differences can create fear: What if we outgrow each other?

Choosing each other in these moments means honoring growth without panic. It means trusting that love can hold difference. It means staying curious instead of threatened.

Choice here looks like:

- listening without judgment

- supporting without controlling

- allowing space without disengaging

- trusting the bond rather than fearing change

Growth does not require separation.

It requires generosity.

Choice and Commitment Are Not the Same Thing

Commitment is the promise you make.

Choice is how you live that promise.

Commitment provides the framework. Choice provides the daily substance. Without choice, commitment becomes obligation. Without commitment, choice becomes fragile.

Healthy relationships hold both.

The Spiritual Weight of Choosing

In Christian theology, love is rarely described as a feeling. It is described as a way of being — patient, kind, faithful, enduring. Love shows up as choice long before it shows up as emotion.

Marriage mirrors this sacred pattern. Choosing each other is not about heroic sacrifice. It's about faithful presence. It's about staying oriented toward love even when the path is unclear.

Every time a couple chooses kindness over contempt, repair over retreat, curiosity over judgment, they participate in holy work.

When One Partner Feels Tired of Choosing

There are moments when one partner feels exhausted — tired of initiating, tired of trying, tired of carrying emotional labor. When this happens, the solution is not blame, but honesty.

Naming fatigue allows the relationship to respond. Ignoring it allows resentment to grow.

Sometimes choosing looks like saying, "I need help choosing right now."

That is not weakness.

It is trust.

Choosing Each Other Over Time

Over decades, couples will choose each other in different ways. The choice may look energetic in one season and quiet in another. It may look confident one year and uncertain the next.

What matters is not intensity, but persistence.

Long love is not dramatic.

It is durable.

Reflection Questions

What does choosing your partner look like in your daily life right now?

Where does choosing feel easy? Where does it feel heavy?

How do you tend to respond when love requires effort?

What small choice could strengthen your connection this week?

How do you experience being chosen by your partner?

Homework for Chapter Twenty-Nine

1. The Choice Inventory

Each partner names one way they feel chosen in the relationship and one way they'd like to feel chosen more clearly.

2. Practice a Daily Choice

Choose one intentional act each day this week that says, "I choose you."

3. A Simple Prayer

"God, help us keep choosing each other with honesty, patience, and love."

Chapter Thirty

LOVE THAT LASTS: A BLESSING FOR THE JOURNEY AHEAD

Every journey needs a moment to pause — not because it's finished, but because it deserves to be named. This chapter is that pause. Not an ending, but a blessing. Not a neat summary, but a sending.

If you've walked through this book together, you've likely recognized pieces of yourselves along the way: moments of closeness and moments of struggle, seasons of joy and seasons of strain, habits you're proud of and patterns you're still working to heal. That recognition matters. It means you've been paying attention.

Love that lasts is not accidental.

It's practiced.

It's chosen.

It's learned over time.

And most of all, it's lived — imperfectly, courageously, and with grace.

The Myth of Arrival

One of the quiet lies many couples absorb is the idea that there's a destination where the work ends — a place where communication is flawless, conflict disappears, intimacy flows effortlessly, and understanding is automatic. But long love doesn't arrive at perfection. It keeps moving.

Marriage is not something you complete.

It's something you inhabit.

There will always be new seasons, new challenges, new joys, new versions of yourselves to learn. The goal is not to reach a point where effort is no longer required. The goal is to become the kind of couple who knows how to keep tending what matters.

Love that lasts is not static.

It is alive.

What You've Been Practicing All Along

Whether you realized it or not, by engaging these chapters together you've already been practicing the core habits of enduring love:

- telling the truth gently

- listening with curiosity

- repairing after conflict

- honoring boundaries

- offering forgiveness without denial

- staying connected during hardship

- choosing each other intentionally

- making room for growth

- tending intimacy with care

- holding faith, doubt, and hope together

These are not "advanced relationship skills."

They are human skills — learned through humility, patience, and courage.

And you will not practice them perfectly.

That's not the expectation.

Grace Is the Atmosphere Love Needs

If there is one thing that sustains long love more than anything else, it is grace — the decision to respond to imperfection with compassion rather than contempt.

Grace understands that people are always in process.

Grace allows space for growth.

Grace softens disappointment.

Grace keeps curiosity alive when frustration would be easier.

Grace says, "We're still learning," instead of, "You should know better by now."

Grace does not excuse harm.

It does not erase accountability.

It does not ignore truth.

Grace creates the conditions where truth can be spoken and healing can happen.

When Love Feels Strong

There will be seasons when love feels light, joyful, and deeply affirming — when laughter comes easily, affection feels natural, and connection flows without effort. In these moments, receive the gift fully.

Celebrate them.

Name them.

Store them gently in memory.

These seasons nourish you for the times when love feels heavier.

When Love Feels Fragile

There will also be seasons when love feels fragile — when stress, exhaustion, grief, or disappointment dulls connection. In those moments, remember this:

Fragility does not mean failure.

It means care is needed.

This is when the practices matter most — slowing down, telling the truth, asking for help, staying emotionally present, choosing repair over retreat. Fragile seasons invite tenderness, not panic.

Love that lasts is not unbreakable.

It is repairable.

You Will Change — and That's the Point

Neither of you will remain exactly who you are today. You will grow. You will heal. You will question. You will discover new parts of yourselves. Sometimes you will surprise each other. Sometimes you will need to reintroduce yourselves.

Healthy love makes room for this.

It says:

"Who you are becoming matters to me."

"Let's learn each other again."

Change does not threaten love.

Refusing to adapt does.

Love Is Not a Role — It's a Relationship

You do not have to perform love correctly.

You do not have to resemble anyone else's marriage.

You do not have to meet anyone else's expectations.

Your relationship is yours.

For some couples, love looks quiet and steady.

For others, playful and expressive.

For others, deeply spiritual.

For others, fiercely practical.

For others, creatively intertwined.

All of these can be sacred.

The measure of love is not style.

It is faithfulness, care, honesty, and mutual dignity.

For Couples Who Are Still Healing

If you are reading this while carrying unresolved pain, disappointment, or fear, know this: healing is not linear, and you are not behind. Love that lasts often grows out of honest reckoning — naming what hurt, grieving what was lost, and choosing what comes next with intention.

You are allowed to take your time.

You are allowed to seek support.

You are allowed to rest.

Staying engaged with the work of love — even imperfectly — is itself an act of hope.

For Couples Who Feel Strong

If your relationship feels strong, grounded, and life-giving right now, receive that with gratitude — not complacency. Strength is not something to protect anxiously; it's something to steward gently.

Strong relationships stay strong because partners remain curious, humble, and attentive. They don't assume closeness will maintain itself. They keep choosing each other with intention.

For Couples Who Are Just Beginning

If you are early in your journey, let this be a gentle reassurance: you do not need to get everything right. What matters most is learning how to talk, how to repair, how to listen, how to stay present, and how to choose love with honesty.

You will make mistakes.

You will grow together.

That's how love becomes real.

Love as a Witness

Every healthy partnership bears quiet witness to the world. In a culture that often treats love as disposable, faithful relationships — queer and straight alike — testify that commitment is still possible, dignity still matters, and grace still works.

Love that lasts becomes a form of resistance against cynicism.

It says:

"People are worth choosing."

"Connection matters."

"Hope is not naïve."

A Final Word About God

If you are reading this through the lens of Christian faith, re-member this: God is not an external judge evaluating your rela-tionship. God is present within it — in your efforts, your failures, your forgiveness, your laughter, your courage, your repair.

God meets you not in perfection, but in love honestly practiced.

And if your faith is still forming, uncertain, or evolving, trust this: love itself is holy ground. Wherever people choose patience, kindness, faithfulness, and care — God is already there.

A Blessing for You Both

May your love be strong enough to tell the truth

and gentle enough to hear it.

May you learn how to fight without wounding

and how to forgive without forgetting your worth.

May your home be a place of safety, laughter, rest, and repair.

May you grow without fear

and change without losing each other.

May you choose one another

not just when it's easy,

but when it's meaningful.

May grace be the atmosphere of your love,

and hope its steady companion.

And when the road feels uncertain,

may you remember this simple truth:

Love matters.

And the way you love each other matters more than you know.

Afterword

Love, Lived in the Real World

If you've made it this far, first of all — well done. That alone says something about you. Not because you finished a book, but because you stayed curious about love. You stayed willing to reflect, to listen, to think honestly about your relationship and yourself. That matters more than most people realize.

This book was never meant to be read quickly or impressively. It was meant to be lived with — slowly, imperfectly, in conversation. It's meant to sit open on a kitchen table, dog-eared and underlined. It's meant to spark conversations that begin with, "Okay, this part made me think..." and sometimes end with, "...and I didn't know how to say that before."

If this book has helped you talk more honestly, listen more carefully, or soften toward each other even once — it has done its job.

Why This Book Exists at All

Let me say something plainly, because honesty matters here.

I did not write this book because I have marriage "figured out."

I wrote it because I have lived it.

I've walked with couples as a pastor.

I've mediated conflict as a director of a Christian conciliation service.

I've listened to stories of love, betrayal, repair, hope, exhaustion, and courage.

I've watched relationships fracture — and I've watched them heal.

And yes — I've been married three times.

That fact alone will disqualify me in some people's minds. Others will read it as a warning label. I understand both reactions. But here's what it's given me that no theory ever could: humility.

I know what it's like to love deeply and fail painfully.

I know what it's like to make vows with sincerity — and still fall short.

I know what it's like to look back and wish I had known then what I know now.

This book is not written from a pedestal.

It's written from the road.

Why Experience Matters More Than Expertise

There are plenty of books written by people who want to tell you how to do marriage correctly. This is not one of them.

This book is written for people who want to do marriage honestly.

People who are learning in real time.

People who love each other but still get stuck.

People who want better tools, not better slogans.

People who are willing to admit, "We're good — but we could be healthier."

People who are thinking, "We're struggling — but we're not done."

Love doesn't need more perfection.

It needs more honesty.

For Every Kind of Couple

This book was written intentionally for every kind of couple.

For straight couples.

For gay and lesbian couples.

For queer, trans, and nonbinary partners.

For couples who look traditional.

For couples who don't.

Love is not owned by one demographic.

Commitment is not the property of one orientation.

Faithfulness is not limited to one expression of partnership.

If your relationship is rooted in mutual dignity, consent, care, and love — this book is for you.

And if you've ever felt excluded, judged, or erased by Christian conversations about marriage, let me say this clearly:

You belong here.

For Couples Just Beginning

If you are early in your relationship, you may be reading this book with excitement, hope, and maybe a little anxiety. That's normal.

Here's what I want you to hear:

You don't need to be afraid of getting it wrong.

You will misunderstand each other.

You will argue about things that later feel ridiculous.

You will say things poorly and mean them well.

You will learn as you go.

The goal is not to avoid mistakes.

The goal is to learn how to repair them.

Start practicing honesty early.

Learn how to apologize sincerely.

Get comfortable naming needs.

Fight fairly.

Laugh often.

Don't keep score.

You're not trying to create a flawless relationship.

You're building a resilient one.

For Couples in the Middle

If you've been together a while, you may have read parts of this book and thought, "Oh. That's us."

The routines.

The stress.

The affection that's still there, but quieter.

The love that's real, but tired sometimes.

That doesn't mean you're failing.

It means you're normal.

Long relationships aren't sustained by intensity.

They're sustained by attention.

Revisit the basics.

Talk again.

Touch more intentionally.

Name appreciation out loud.

Repair faster.

Assume goodwill.

And remember this:

The middle chapters of a love story are where depth is built.

For Couples Who Are Struggling

If you're reading this because something feels fragile — please know this:

Struggle does not mean your relationship is over.

It means it needs care.

Some of the strongest relationships I've ever encountered were forged in seasons of deep difficulty. Not because pain is good, but because honesty was finally unavoidable.

If you're stuck:

get help sooner rather than later

don't wait until resentment calcifies

don't confuse pride with strength

don't isolate

Counseling is not failure.

Pastoral support is not weakness.

Learning new skills is not an admission of defeat.

It's an act of love.

For Pastors, Counselors, and Friends Who Care

If you are using this book as a resource — with couples in your church, in counseling settings, or simply because you care about someone's relationship — thank you.

We need fewer voices offering judgment and more offering wisdom.

Fewer quick answers and more patient listening.

Fewer rigid formulas and more compassionate tools.

This book was designed to be used, not admired.

To be discussed, not skimmed.

To be a companion, not a rulebook.

What I Hope You Take With You

If this book leaves you with nothing else, I hope it leaves you with these truths:

Love is learned, not mastered

Conflict is not the enemy — contempt is

Repair matters more than perfection

Growth is uneven and that's okay

Forgiveness is a process, not a switch

Intimacy evolves and can deepen

Boundaries protect love, they don't threaten it

Choosing each other is a daily practice

Grace makes everything possible

And perhaps most importantly:

Love is worth the work.

Not because it's always easy.

But because it shapes who we become.

A Final Blessing

May you keep telling the truth — kindly.

May you listen without defensiveness.

May you forgive without erasing yourself.

May you fight fairly and repair gently.

May you laugh often and rest well.

May your love grow wiser with time.

And when you stumble — because you will —

may you remember that stumbling is not the opposite of love.

Indifference is.

So stay engaged.

Stay curious.

Stay tender.

Love matters.

And the way you practice it matters more than you know.

About the Author

About the Author

Mark David Albertson is a pastor, writer, and longtime guide for couples navigating love, conflict, and commitment in the real world.

He has served as a pastor and as Director of a Christian Conciliation service, has given more than 1000 seminars and workshops, and has spent a lifetime walking with couples through seasons of deep connection, painful conflict, honest repair, and hopeful rebuilding. His work is shaped by progressive Christian theology, a deep respect for human dignity, and the conviction that relationships grow best through grace rather than fear.

Mark is also a novelist and teacher, known for weaving story, humor, and practical wisdom together in ways that feel accessible and deeply human. He brings both professional experience and personal humility to his writing, openly acknowledging his own complicated journey through love and marriage. Mark hosts two YouTube series, "Faith on the Farm," with his wife, Kaia as they negotiate faith and farm in the Pacific Northwest, and "Making Time for God," video teachings on a variety of subjects.

Love Matters was written not from a pedestal, but from the road — as a resource for couples, pastors, counselors, and anyone who believes that love is worth tending with honesty, patience, and care.

To learn more about Mark, you can visit his website www.pro gressivepreacher.com

Also by Mark David Albertson

Inspiration

Love Made Flesh: Reflections on the Meaning of Christmas

Bible Studies

The Gospel of John

The Gospel of Mark

The Book of James

Faith in Action

Jesus and Social Justice

Novels

Steaming: A Sea Story

Spying: A Sea Story

Stalking: A Sea Story

Jemez

The Just (2026)